About the Author

John McCormick is a visiting assistant professor of political science at Indiana University–Purdue University at Indianapolis (IUPUI) in the United States.

A specialist in environmental policy and West European politics, he has degrees from the University of London and Indiana University. He worked during the early 1980s for the World Wide Fund for Nature and IIED in London, and has published widely on environmental politics. His most recent books were *Acid Earth: The Global Threat of Acid Pollution* (Earthscan, 1989) and *The Global Environment Movement* (Belhaven Press, 1989; published in the United States as *Reclaiming Paradise*).

British Politics and the Environment

John McCormick

Earthscan Publications Ltd, London

First published 1991 by
Earthscan Publications Ltd
3 Endsleigh Street, London WC1H 0DD

British Library Cataloguing in Publication Data:
McCormick, John
British Politics and the Environment
1. Great Britain. Environment. Policies of government
I. Title
333.70941

ISBN 1-85383-090-9

Production by Bob Towell
Typeset by Rapid Communications Ltd, Bristol
Printed and bound by Cox & Wyman Ltd

Earthscan Publications Ltd is an editorially independent subsidiary of the International Institute for Environment and Development (Charity No. 800066)

Contents

Acronyms

CAP	Common Agricultural Policy
CEGB	Central Electricity Generating Board
CLA	Country Landowners Association
CLEAR	Campaign for Lead-Free Air
CPRE	Council for the Protection of Rural England
DOE	Department of the Environment
EC	European Community
EEB	European Environmental Bureau
FOE	Friends of the Earth
FWAG	Farming and Wildlife Advisory Group
HMIP	Her Majesty's Inspectorate of Pollution
IEEP	Institute for European Environmental Policy
MAFF	Ministry of Agriculture, Food and Fisheries
NCC	Nature Conservancy Council
NERC	Natural Environment Research Council
NFU	National Farmers Union
NGO	non-governmental organization
NRA	National Rivers Authority
NSCA	National Society for Clean Air
PWR	pressurized-water reactor
RCEP	Royal Commission on Environmental Pollution
RSPB	Royal Society for the Protection of Birds
RWA	Regional Water Authority
WWF	World Wide Fund for Nature (formerly World Wildlife Fund)
CFCs	chlorofluorocabons
CO_2	carbon dioxide
NO_x	nitrogen oxide
SO_2	sulphur dioxide

Introduction

In May 1979, Margaret Thatcher came to power on a platform aimed at reviving the British economy, curing the "British disease", reducing the welfare state, and encouraging fundamental changes in the economic and social assumptions of British society. Over the course of three administrations, she set out to create an enterprise culture, to reduce central planning and regulation, to reduce the role of government in business and industry, and to leave the allocation of resources and decisions on prices and wages to the free market. Many of her policies were based on a single key principle: a dislike of consensus politics, and opposition to the idea that government should rule through compromise, including giving an ear to the demands of interest groups.

Mrs Thatcher also came to power with little interest in environmental issues, and little understanding of environmental problems. In a now famous statement at the time of the Falklands crisis, she described the environment as a "humdrum" issue. Her low interest in the environment was little different from that of her predecessors; Britain in 1979 had no environmental policy, and few people in government really understood what the environment was all about. Where it was mentioned at all in the major party manifestos, it was narrowly defined, and low on the agenda. Where Mrs Thatcher even thought about the environment during her first two administrations, she was unsympathetic to the demands of British environmental groups. Not only did reference to the environmental lobby smack of consensus and compromise, but she was ideologically opposed to the arguments of most environmental groups that more government regulation was essential if Britain was to avoid continued environmental degradation.

Against this background, it was all the more surprising when Mrs Thatcher, in speeches in September and October 1988, spoke of nurturing and safeguarding the environment, declared that protecting the balance of nature was "one of the great challenges of the late twentieth century", and described the Conservative Party as "friends of the Earth". Four months before, after nearly a decade of intransigence, she had finally committed Britain to an expensive programme to reduce acid rain. Following her autumn speeches, she took an increasingly public and outspoken role in encouraging action on avoiding global warming and protecting the ozone layer; this included her leading role in the February 1989 London conference on the ozone layer. In late 1989, the government announced that it would draw up a white paper on the environment; this was finally published in September 1990.

What were the motives behind this apparently dramatic conversion? Was there in fact such a conversion? How did such pro-environmental statements sit against a background of ardently anti-regulation Thatcherism, a strong belief in conviction politics and a rejection of compromise? Were these statements an indication of the growing power of the environmental lobby, or were they simply indicators of Thatcherite pragmatism? Was the British government finally giving due attention to the environment and the need for a rational environmental policy?

Whatever the motives, there is little doubt that the third Thatcher administration saw the environment leap to the highest reaches of the British public policy agenda. In the summer of 1989, Britain and the British seemed to have gone green. People were talking about buying green products in the supermarket, seeking out organic food, looking for local recycling schemes, converting their cars to run on unleaded petrol and worrying about how their way of life was contributing to global warming and destruction of the tropical rain forests. Phrases like "ozone-friendly", "chemical-free", "biodegradable", "not tested on animals" and "environmentally friendly" began to pepper the products on supermarket shelves. Environmental groups were awash with new membership applications, requests for information, and money. The Greens signed up hundreds of new members every month, and in June 1989 surprised everyone with a 15 per cent share of the vote in the European elections. Mrs Thatcher appointed a new and more sympathetic environment secretary, and chaired a cabinet committee set up to produce the white paper on the environment. In public opinion polls, the environment repeatedly came out as one of the two or three most prominent issues on people's minds.

British Politics and the Environment is an attempt to understand and explain these changes. It is a portrait of environmental politics in Britain during the 1980s, a time of great change in British society. It is based on the premise that British governments have traditionally cared and understood little about the environment as either a policy issue or a political issue, and that protection of the environment is undertaken mainly by a voluntary environmental lobby consisting of many different interest groups and millions of members. It argues that the environmental lobby is the only real opposition to the government when it comes to the environment, and that environmental policy in Britain is made mainly as a result of conflict (and sometimes compromise) between the lobby and the government. It looks at that relationship, at the changes that took place in the environmental lobby during the 1980s and at the changing place of the environment on the public policy agenda.

At the same time, *British Politics and the Environment* is an attempt to contribute to the broader discussion about the nature of Thatcherism, its short- and long-term effects on British politics and the place of interest groups in British politics. It uses the experience of the environmental lobby to test Mrs Thatcher's claims to have abandoned consensus politics and to have governed Britain on the basis of personal and ideological convictions. Has Thatcherism really brought a permanent change to the style of British government, and to the relationship between government and interest groups?

Although there are about 150 organizations which can be described as national, regional or local environmental interest groups, *British Politics and the Environment* pays particular attention to the work of seven of the biggest and/or most consistently influential of the national groups: the Council for the Protection of Rural England, Friends of the Earth, the Green Alliance, Greenpeace, the National Trust, the Royal Society for the Protection of Birds and the World Wide Fund for Nature.

Chapter 1 looks at the environment as a policy issue, and at its place in the policy process in Britain. It describes how environmental policy is made in Britain, and discusses the role of interest groups in the policy process. Chapter 2 then looks at the environmental lobby, describing its history and character, analysing its structure, methods and goals in the early 1980s and assessing its relationship with the members and institutions of government. Chapter 3 is an assessment of Thatcherism. What were Mrs Thatcher's attitudes during the 1980s to consensus politics, interest groups and the environment, and how did her policies on the environment evolve?

The next four chapters examine specific elements of environmental policy, and how approaches to them have changed. Chapter 4 begins with an analysis of the countryside issue, together with an assessment of the role of environmental groups in influencing countryside policy. It looks at the rise of the conservation debate, the decline of the farming lobby and the growing impact of conservation groups. Chapter 5 looks at the new prominence of pollution issues in the late 1980s, and at the interplay between environmental groups, the privatization of the water and electricity supply industries and the new prominence of global issues. Chapter 6 looks at the green consumer revolution, and at the rise of green politics in Britain and Europe. Chapter 7 examines the impact of the European Community on environmental policy in Britain, and the effect this has had on the British government, and on the tactics and power of the environmental lobby.

Chapter 8 describes the changes that took place in the environmental lobby during the 1980s, and looks at the structure and influence of the lobby today. Finally, Chapter 9 asks what has happened to the environment as a policy issue, and what the changes that have taken place in the goals, methods and influence of environmental groups in Britain say about the nature of British government, and about the place of the environment in British politics.

British Politics and the Environment began life as a doctoral thesis in political science, written at Indiana University in the United States. In writing it, I drew on my own experience of the British environmental lobby in the early 1980s, and my time on the staff of the World Wildlife Fund (1980-81) and the International Institute for Environment and Development (1982-6). I also spent part of the summers of 1989 and 1990 collecting data from groups and interviewing members and observers of the environmental lobby.

I would like to thank a number of people for their help. Jim Christoph was a concerned and diligent chairman of my doctoral committee, who kept track of every stage of the development of the thesis, and played a key role in setting its direction and guiding its development. The remaining members of the committee provided much useful guidance: Professors Lynton Caldwell, J. Gus Liebenow and Richard Stryker.

Philip Lowe was supervisor of my master's thesis at the University of London, and has given me enormous help over the years. His research on environmental politics in Britain in the last decade has been ground-breaking, and he freely shared with me his thoughts on the changes that took place under Thatcherism. In a sense, this book takes up and continues some of the ideas raised in his work with Jane Goyder on environmental groups in the early 1980s, published as *Environmental Groups in Politics* (London: Allen & Unwin, 1983).

Finally, I owe a debt to the staff of the organizations which provided so much of the information that forms the basis of this book. The new prominence of environmentalism in Britain has not only made most of the groups much busier, but has also increased the volume of requests for information from people like me. Despite that, all but two of the groups I approached proved enormously helpful, and more than willing to answer my questions.

For giving up time to talk to me about their work and the state of environmental politics in Britain today, I would like to thank Bill Adams (Downing College, Cambridge), David Baldock (Institute for European Environmental Policy), Tim Brown (National Society for Clean Air), Tom Burke (Green Alliance), Heather Corrie (World Wide Fund for Nature), John Elkington (SustainAbility), Alistair Gammell (Royal Society for the Protection of Birds), Nigel Haigh (Institute for European Environmental Policy), Peter McDonald (Wildlife Link), George Medley (World Wide Fund for Nature), Emma Louise O'Reilly (National Trust), Jonathon Porritt (former director, Friends of the Earth), Chris Rose (Media Natura), Chris Tydeman (World Wide Fund for Nature) and Andy Wilson (Council for the Protection of Rural England).

For providing information or corresponding with me on the work of their respective organizations, I would like to thank Ivan Hattingh and Sarah King (World Wide Fund for Nature), Stuart Housden (Royal Society for the Protection of Birds), Sara Huey and Tanya Morrison (Friends of the Earth), Alan Mattingly (Ramblers' Association) and Peter Melchett (Greenpeace).

With their help, I hope I have written a book that will encourage more people to think about the political dimensions of the environment, and will encourage more political scientists to give the environment the attention it deserves in their writing and research on public policy in Britain.

1. Environmental Policy in Britain

By almost every measure, the environment is a relatively minor issue on the British political agenda. Political debates in Britain usually centre on foreign policy, defence, social security, home affairs, education, housing, industry and economic policy; rarely do they touch on the environment. The same goes for the literature on British politics; a search through all the standard studies of British politics – and through the recent torrent of studies of Thatcher and Thatcherism – reveals little beyond passing references to the environment. A recent collection of essays on Thatcherism mentions the environment as a postscript to housing, devoting just over three pages out of 355 to the topic.[1] Where environmental policy is discussed by politicians and political scientists, it is regularly misunderstood and misdefined. One recent definition is both limited and outdated: "[policy] concerned with the use of land and the regulation of human activities which have an impact on our physical surroundings".[2]

This chapter must begin, then, with a clear definition of public policy and environmental policy. For present purposes, public policy is defined as the actions of government; in other words, everything that governments do or might do. Environmental policy is defined as public policy concerned with governing the relationship between people and their natural environment. The emphasis here is on people as part of a natural system (unlike the British government and many political scientists, I exclude the built environment). Ideally, the goal of environmental policy should be to maximize the welfare of people and their environment, and to ensure that all development (economic, social and/or political) is sustainable. It should address the needs of the "human environment", and should take a holistic view of the place of human society in the world.

The issues that concern environmental policy-makers change with time and place. For example, in "developing" countries, the environment as an issue usually involves such problems as soil erosion, desertification, deforestation, fuelwood shortages, rapid population growth and the destruction of wildlife. All of these are problems which are ultimately linked to poverty. In other words, many of their basic causes lie in poverty, and their effects include the promotion of more poverty, particularly in rural areas. In "communist" countries, the problems are different. While the Soviet Union and Eastern Europe were still centrally planned, most environmental problems (notably pollution) were the result of inefficient planning, an emphasis on industrial and agricultural development at almost any cost, an incompetent bureaucracy and technological hubris.

In industrialized liberal democracies, meanwhile, the environment usually covers such issues as waste, air and water pollution, commercial energy management, recycling, the battle between using and conserving resources and the spread of urban areas. These are all problems which are ultimately linked to excessive and careless consumption. Even *among* industrialized countries, the issues differ. In the United States, the important problems are how to dispose of toxic wastes, and how to manage the exploitation of public lands. In Britain, there is an emphasis on the health of the countryside, and maintaining a balance between farming and wildife. At the same time, both countries have common problems, such as air and water pollution.

Principles of British environmental policy

Britain has a curious approach to environmental management,

one that appears at first sight to be full of contradictions. On the one hand, the British people value their countryside, wildlife, scenic beauty, city parks, gardens and country estates. The study of natural history is a popular pastime, and Britain has produced many great naturalists, from Gilbert White through Alfred Russell Wallace to Charles Darwin, Julian Huxley and Peter Scott. Britain also has had an impressive record in recognizing and responding to environmental degradation.

- In 1273, Britain passed what may have been the world's first piece of anti-pollution legislation (a decree prohibiting the burning of sea coal).
- In 1863, Britain created the world's first government environmental agency, the Alkali Inspectorate. The job of the Inspectorate was to regulate the emission of acid fumes from the alkali industry, which made sodium carbonate, used in the manufacture of soap, glass and textiles.
- The Commons, Open Spaces and Footpaths Preservation Society – founded in 1865 – was the world's first private environmental group.
- In 1947, Britain passed one of the most comprehensive planning Acts in the world, the Town and Country Planning Act.
- The world's first comprehensive air pollution control Act was the Clean Air Act of 1956, which predated similar legislation in most other liberal democracies.
- In 1970, Britain created the world's first cabinet-level environment department.

This is an impressive record, but milestones like these have to be seen against an underlying record of what might variously be described as environmental lethargy, apathy or ignorance on the part of successive British governments. Particularly since the Second World War, they have proved slow to recognize and understand the environment as a distinct policy area, slow to tighten environmental legislation, unwilling to provide environmental agencies with adequate power or funding, loath to support international attempts to control acid pollution or prevent the dumping of toxic wastes at sea and reluctant to reform agricultural policy in such a way as to protect Britain's countryside.

Britain's position on acid pollution provides a good example of the contradictions. The problem was first identified in Britain in the 1850s;[3] Battersea power-station in London (opened in 1929) was the first power-station in the world to fit anti-pollution scrubbers; and London was one of the first cities in the world to respond successfully to smog problems. Yet, when acid pollution was finally recognized as an urgent international problem in the 1980s, and when the Scandinavians and the West Germans began taking action to curb acid pollution, Britain demurred.[4] It was only in 1988 – long after all its European partners had agreed to act, and *then* only as a result of a European Community directive on large sources of pollution – that the British government finally agreed to reduce emissions of the sulphur dioxide and nitrogen oxides that cause acid pollution.

There are several possible explanations for this strangely paradoxical record. First, the environment as a policy area has not only been misunderstood by British governments, but it has also been particularly prone to the kind of *ad hoc*, improvisational and piecemeal responses that characterize the policy process generally, in Britain as elsewhere. This is a classic example of what the American political economist Charles Lindblom calls "disjointed incrementalism". Policy-makers do not always approach public policy methodically. Instead, they often make decisions through small or incremental moves on particular problems rather than through a comprehensive reform programme.[5] Not only has this led to a lack of direction in environmental policy-making, but it has left Britain with a confused and confusing medley of institutions and laws. Britain has no such thing as a coherent and recognizable environmental policy. As Lowe and Flynn argue:

> government structures and law relating to environmental protection have been (and largely remain) an accretion of common law,

> statutes, agencies, procedures and policies. There is no overall environmental policy other than the sum of these individual elements, most of which have been pragmatic and incremental responses to specific problems and the evolution of relevant scientific knowledge.[6]

Secondly, public policy in Britain is normally worked out through a process that emphasizes consensus and consultation with affected interests. Jordan and Richardson argue that "most political activity is bargained in private worlds by special interests and interested specialists".[7] British policy-makers often think of themselves as custodians of the public interest, and feel that they can understand the best interests of the public with minimal reference to the public itself. One of the characteristics of British politics is secrecy; the government limits public access to information in the belief that a passive public will accept what the government thinks is in the public interest.

The result of this is that much of Britain's regulatory policy-making is designed and carried out by selective consultation with interest groups. Neither the regulators nor the industries being regulated feel any need or requirement to let the public know what they are doing. The most influential voice in the making of a new law is often the lobby or the economic sector being regulated by that new law. Poachers and gamekeepers work closely together to decide what each finds acceptable. In the case of the environment, environmental groups – which have regularly pushed for more and stronger regulation – have usually ended up having less influence on how policy is made than the industrialists, farmers and others who are supposedly being regulated.

Under these circumstances, it follows that some interests will have their demands met more successfully than others, and that the resulting body of laws will be incomplete and have varied effectiveness. The consultation that has traditionally taken place between the regulators and the regulated – and the relative powers of regulated interests and the environmental lobby – is exemplified by the 1974 Control of Pollution Act, which was essentially shaped by industry and local government, despite more than 150 amendments tabled by environmental interest groups.[8] Similarly, the 1981 Wildlife and Countryside Act, one of the most controversial and influential pieces of legislation affecting rural scenery and semi-natural wildlife habitats, was largely shaped by the powerful farming and landowning lobbies, despite more than 2,300 amendments tabled by wildlife and landscape interest groups, among others. Environmental groups have had to compete with other interests with a lot more influence in the corridors of government, such as the farming lobby and the nuclear power industry. More recently, they have had to face up to the additional challenge of the uncompromising Thatcherite commitment to economic growth, supported by business, industry and the trade unions.

Nowhere is the unwillingness of the government to use coercion better exemplified than in pollution control. In countries like the United States and Germany, pollution policy is based on setting agreed standards and targets. In Britain, the government has traditionally relied almost entirely on encouraging industry to comply voluntarily with "decent" standards of behavior. Pollution control laws tend to be broad and discretionary, and the regulatory agencies are usually given wide scope to establish and enforce environmental objectives.

This all ties in with the notion of the Nanny State, first described by Jon Tinker in 1972, when he suggested that the government relied for its pollution control objectives on appeals to the sense of fair play of polluting industries. Some of Britain's pollution rules, he argued, were better suited to an Edwardian girls' school than to an advanced industrial society. Offenders, he noted, were "taken quietly on one side by the prefects and ticked off for letting the side down. There is no need for prosecutions: the shame of being found out is reckoned to be punishment enough."[9] It was a question of Nanny knowing best. This non-coercive approach to pollution control is reflected in the fact that the Alkali Inspectorate prosecuted just three cases between 1920 and 1967. Polluters are regarded as innocent until proven guilty. In 1972, the Royal Commission on Environmental Pollution concluded in its second annual report that there was a need for more public openness in the environmental policy process.[10]

The third possible explanation for the paradoxes in British environmental policy is the high level of devolved and decentralized authority in Britain. Local government has traditionally been responsible for environmental regulation, but relatively few people have much interest in local politics, so local authorities are not made accountable. To complicate the picture, there is the economic factor: in the traditional industrial heartlands of the Midlands, the North, South Wales and Scotland, the weakness of local government has been reinforced by a prevailing public unwillingness to support the expense of controlling pollution. In coal-mining areas particularly, local people have been unwilling to accept less pollutive alternative energy sources, such as natural gas. As has been the case so often elsewhere, the concern is that environmental controls will undermine existing industry and drive away new industry at a time of economic hardship.

Public campaigns to control pollution have been further handicapped by the fact that pollution simply hasn't been much of a public issue. Certainly it has been less of an issue than the protection of the countryside. Perhaps many people felt that the Clean Air Act had done its work; and as far as water was concerned, most people seemed convinced that it was clean. The picture changed in 1989. With her plans to privatize the electricity and water supply industries, Mrs Thatcher achieved the unintentional and unanticipated effect of making pollution a major public issue, of exposing existing pollution control practices to their most searching public scrutiny, and of making people aware – many for the first time – that Britain's air and water were not as clean as widely thought (see Chapter 5).

The pitfalls of policy-making

At the best of times, making and implementing public policy is an enormously complex affair. The more complex the issue, the more confusing the process. In almost any area of policy, there are many different actors, processes and pressures involved, and the network of government agencies set up to respond is usually confused and confusing. It is frequently difficult to be sure exactly who is responsible. Nowhere is this more obvious than in environmental policy. The confusion has several possible causes.

First, the environment – perhaps more than any other area of public policy except economic or foreign policy – is difficult to compartmentalize. It overlaps with almost every other policy area, from science and technology to industry, agriculture, energy, trade, transportation, health, recreation and economic and foreign policy. This makes the delineation of departmental responsibilities very difficult. Simply setting up an environmental protection agency and letting it develop from there is not the end of the problem. Because of the complexity of the environment as a policy issue, environmental ministries or agencies often have to interfere with (and sometimes police) the activities of other ministries and agencies. This can lead to institutional jealousy and resentment, and to hamstrung environmental agencies.

Secondly, the environment is a relative newcomer to the policy agenda. Not only do environmental agencies usually have to compete for funds and power as junior partners in government, but they are also in an early stage of evolution. Between 1863 (when the British Alkali Inspectorate was created) and 1971, only twelve countries created national environmental agencies. Since 1972, almost every other country has created such an agency. So, in most cases, environmental agencies have had less than twenty years to develop a base of support and to work out a set of priorities, goals and methods.

Their lack of success is in turn complicated by the fact that the causes, effects and cures of environmental problems are still so poorly understood. This is the case in almost every area of environmental policy, from land management to air and water pollution, toxic wastes and energy policy. Nowhere is this more obvious than in the controversy over global warming. Is the global climate really changing? If so, what is causing that change? If the change is caused by human activities, how can it be stopped? This lack of certainty and understanding has often been used by governments as an argument – some would say an excuse – for caution in approaching environmental issues. Without an understanding of the nature and parameters of environmental problems, environmental agencies and the laws they design must almost inevitably be handicapped. Given that so much is still being learned about the causes and consequences of environmental problems, it is hardly surprising that so many environmental agencies are small, underfunded and lacking real direction.

Finally, because the environment has been such a minor issue on the British policy agenda, relatively little time and thought have been expended on designing an effective and rational institutional and legislative structure. Repeated calls for institutional reform during the early 1980s (mainly from the environmental lobby and opposition parties) were consistently ignored. Nothing was done about reforming water pollution control, for example, until Mrs Thatcher was compelled to set up a new regulatory agency in 1989 as a result of European Community law.

Who makes environmental policy?

Against this confusing background, it is difficult to say exactly who is responsible for making and implementing environmental policy in Britain. The Department of the Environment, the Nature Conservancy Council, the Countryside Commission and Her Majesty's Inspectorate of Pollution would – if their names are any indication – seem to be centrally involved. At the same time, there are many agencies which are less obviously involved, yet which undertake activities with environmental implications. Among these are British Rail, the British Tourist Authority, the British Waterways Board, the Office of Electricity Regulation, the National Rivers Authority and the Health and Safety Executive. In addition, the fact that the government has been relatively lethargic in its response to environmental problems has meant that much practical environmental management, fund-raising and public education is undertaken by the environmental lobby: voluntary agencies, lobbying groups, charities, interest groups and private research institutions.

Until 1970, authority for environmental regulation in Britain was divided among a mixed bag of agencies. Responsibility for air pollution control was divided among the ministries of transport, housing, local government, technology and agriculture, the Department of Social Services, the Board of Trade and the secretaries of state for Scotland and Wales. Harold Wilson first proposed a reorganization of environmental agencies in 1969, and created both the Ministry for Local Government and Regional Planning and the Royal Commission on Environmental Pollution. There was much discussion about environmental issues within both the Labour government and the Conservative opposition in 1969–70, and some thought that the environment might be an election issue for the first time in 1970. In the end, the closeness of the election encouraged both major parties to focus on more familiar issues.

Following the Conservative victory, the word "environment" appeared for the first time in the Queen's Speech in July 1970. In October, the reorganization of government machinery planned by the Wilson government was outlined in a government white paper. The Heath administration had a predilection for institutional reform and the creation of new "super-agencies", the goal being to promote central control. In line with this, the ministries of housing and local government, public building and works, and transport were amalgamated in 1970 into a new Department of the Environment (DOE), responsible for "the whole range of functions which affect people's living environment".

Despite its name, the creation of the DOE was more a reorganization of government machinery than the creation of a new department with new powers. Many key environmental concerns were left with other departments. For example, responsibility for energy supply, a fundamental aspect of environmental policy, remained with the Department of Energy and the Central Electricity Generating Board. Until the appointment of Chris Patten as environment secretary in 1989, no environment secretary had shown any particular interest in the environment. The very title Department of the "Environment" was misleading, because environmental policy proved to be a small (and not very important) part of its responsibilities. As of February 1989, about 10 per cent of the staff of the department actually dealt with environmental issues, rather than housing or local government.[11] The department has responsibilities from planning to local government, housing, inner-city issues, sport and recreation, royal parks and ancient monuments. It has given most of its attention to local government and housing. In late 1989 and early 1990, most of its time was spent dealing with the implementation of the new community charge; this remained the priority of Michael Heseltine in 1991 on his return to the DOE.

The DOE is responsible in turn for the two state conservation agencies – the Nature Conservancy Council and the Countryside Commission. The Nature Conservancy Council (NCC) is the state wildlife conservation agency. Created as the National Parks Commission under the National Parks and Access to the Countryside Act of 1949, the NCC was later renamed the Nature Conservancy, and given its present title in 1973, when many of its research functions were split off into the Institute of Terrestrial Ecology. The NCC has a staff of more than a thousand and an annual budget of £44 million.

In 1980, the Council was widely regarded among environmental groups as ineffective, powerless and secretive, and as being slow to speak out against the destruction of sites of natural interest and value by farming and forestry activities. It was also regularly criticized for having a leadership dominated by career civil servants, foresters, farmers and industrialists. A former chairman, Sir Ralph Verney, had previously been a Forestry Commissioner and president of the Country Landowners' Association, both organizations which frequently disagree with environmental groups.

The Countryside Commission was similarly criticized. There are two separate Commissions, for England and Wales, and for Scotland. The former has a staff of 150 and an annual budget of £25 million. Created in 1967 (Scotland) and 1968 (England and Wales), the Commissions are responsible for amenity. They own no land, but are charged with helping design policy on national parks (except in Scotland), providing grants for public access to open countryside, and helping create country parks and designating Areas of Outstanding Natural Beauty, Heritage Coasts and (in Scotland) National Scenic Areas. The Commissions have an advisory role, and may be consulted by public and private landowners on amenity questions. The Commissions were often accused by environmental groups of being dominated by the interests of commercial agriculture and forestry. Repeated suggestions were made during the 1970s and 1980s for an amalgamation of the NCC and the Countryside Commissions.[12]

Relations between the environmental lobby and the state agencies have improved in recent years. The Council and the Commissions have been seen to be more critical of government policy and more willing to resist that policy. When plans were proposed by the Thatcher administration in July 1989 to dismember the state agencies and create separate bodies for Scotland and Wales, the opposition of the environmental lobby was instant, unanimous and vocal. "The announcement outraged the conservation movement," noted the CPRE in its annual report.[13] There was a suspicion among environmental groups that the two agencies had become too effective at slowing down the conversion of natural habitat to farmland, and fears that the dismemberment plans were intended to weaken the powers of the agencies.

The DOE is also responsible for Her Majesty's Inspectorate of Pollution (HMIP). Created in 1987 in an attempt to establish a unified approach to pollution abatement, the goal of HMIP is to make sure that every large emission source is regulated by a single inspector. The inspector's responsibility is to find the "best practicable environmental option" (BPEO) for the disposal of effluent. The BPEO concept was in turn developed by the Royal Commission on Environmental Pollution (RCEP), created in 1970. The notion of the Royal Commission – an advisory committee appointed by the government to investigate and report on a particular problem – is peculiarly British. The RCEP has no executive functions, but plays a purely advisory role. Despite this, its annual reports have often had a major influence on the public debate about pollution.

This pot-pourri of environmental agencies has undergone some fundamental changes since 1987, not because the government has recognized the weakness of the existing system, but because of economic and legal concerns over the arrangements made for controlling pollution from the newly privatized electricity and water supply industries. Mrs Thatcher had originally proposed allowing the privatized water industry to regulate its own pollution emissions, but this was found to be illegal under European Community law, and a new National Rivers Authority was created in 1989 to oversee water pollution control. Similarly, when the electricity supply industry was privatized, a new Office of Electricity Regulation (Offer) was given responsibilities for pollution control and environmental management. Offer has a similar relationship to the privatized electricity supply companies as Oftel has to the privatized British Telecom and Ofgas has to British Gas.

Although at first glance it may not appear to be an environmental agency, the Ministry of Agriculture, Fisheries and Food (MAFF) plays a central role in British environmental policy. The only government department still officially designated as a ministry, MAFF has traditionally focused on encouraging food production. It has also been the subject of repeated criticism by environmental groups for pursuing policies aimed at improving the efficiency and productivity of agriculture at the cost of Britain's natural heritage, notably woodlands and hedgerows. In recent years, MAFF has come to see itself increasingly as a ministry for the countryside, and has been active in assessing countryside issues, notably through its study *Alternative Land Uses and the Rural Economy* (*ALURE*; see Chapter 4).

The work of at least three other departments – trade and industry, energy, and education and science – impinges on environmental matters. For example, the Natural Environment Research Council (NERC), which undertakes research on the natural environment and natural resources as a basis for government policy-making, comes under the aegis of the Department of Education and Science. (Among the NERC's research groups is the Institute of Terrestrial Ecology.) The Forestry Commission is responsible to the Minister of Agriculture in England, and to the secretaries of state for Scotland and Wales. In addition to promoting "the interests of forestry", the development of afforestation and the supply of timber and forest products, the Commission (created in 1919) is responsible for overseeing forestry and forestry research. It also works with the NERC to monitor the effects of pollution on forests. The Commission has been criticized in the past by some environmental groups for suggesting that the interests of commercial forestry and wildlife conservation are compatible, for providing grant aid for the removal of ancient woodland and for promoting fast-growing commercial conifer plantations.[14]

Against a background of variable government interest in environmental regulation, the role and influence of the European Community in environmental policy-making has grown. In fact, it is now arguably the single most important and effective influence on British environmental policy and politics (see Chapter 7). Initially, the Community had no environmental policies of its own. Since the influential 1972 United Nations Conference on the Human Environment, however, it has published a series of four environmental action plans. The Single European Act of 1986 institutionalized this by giving the EC more specific powers over environmental protection.

Among the different means by which the EC enacts its policies, the most important is the European Commission Directive. Directives require member states to create or amend national law according to how they believe they can best meet the purpose of a Directive. As with all Directives, the main goal of environmental Directives is to standardize legislation throughout the Community, and to make sure that environmental regulation is equally applied, irrespective of local priorities and values. Despite its reservations, the Thatcher government found itself obliged to agree with environmental Directives, and accordingly amended domestic policy. For example, it was obliged in 1981 to pass the Wildlife and Countryside Act to meet the terms of the EC Directive on wild birds. It was obliged in 1988 to reverse its opposition to acid pollution control because of the EC Directive on large combustion plants. It was obliged in 1989 to create the National Rivers Authority because, under Community law, it was illegal to place pollution control in the hands of private companies.

Interest groups and policy-making

British government has long worked on the basis that elected officials will be helped, advised and criticized in various ways by interest groups of various kinds. As Dennis Kavanagh puts it:

> consultation with affected and recognized interests is a cultural norm in British government. . . . A group expects to be consulted, almost as of right and certainly as a courtesy, about the details of any forthcoming government legislation and administrative change that is likely to affect it.[15]

This has been particularly true of trade unions and business and economic interests.

Jordan and Richardson suggest that interest groups are the most significant medium for the articulation of society's demands, and "consultation the technique for their amelioration".[16] They argue that interest group activity is "normal, commonplace, unavoidable, and normally desirable", and that in Britain "the incorporation of some types of groups into the process by which policies are formulated and implemented has become routinized in a complex web of informal and formal arrangements".[17]

Samuel Beer writes of his belief that modern British politics is driven by a notion of "collectivism", where the community is "divided into various strata, regards each of these strata as having a certain corporate unity, and holds that they ought to be represented in government".[18] He argues that Britain at the turn of the century saw signs of a general shift in the climate of opinion towards legitimizing functional groups (particularly producer groups), or what amounted to a "new pluralism".[19]

Jordan and Richardson list several important ways in which groups can influence public policy: government departments can allow groups influence in return for information; groups can mobilize public or parliamentary protest of the kind which leaders would rather avoid; legislation can be improved through advice provided by affected groups; and groups can be recruited as allies of government departments, thereby helping those departments to pursue their goals in other ways. Overall, they argue, there is a belief that policies are only defensible when applied with the consent of interested parties.[20]

This latter point raises one of the key questions about government in Britain: can British governments pursue their own coherent, long-term sets of policies, or do they have to compromise by consulting with interest groups? The answer depends on the groups in question. Groups and lobbies differ not only in their size, strength and resources, but also in their standing in public and political opinion. In other words, not all interests carry equal weight or prominence in the political agenda. Their strength and influence obviously affect their access to decision-makers. Environmental groups have traditionally had much less influence on government than economic interest groups, such as trade unions. David Marsh argues that there are a limited number of powerful economic groups which enjoy a privileged position in the decision-making process.[21] Wynn Grant makes a distinction between "insider" and "outsider" groups – the former are accepted as "responsible" groups that can be consulted on a regular basis.[22]

Jordan and Richardson argue that there has been a shift during the twentieth century (especially since the Second World War) towards a much closer integration of groups in the process of policy implementation.[23] Hood argues that much of the growth in government has not been in central government departments, but in "indirect government". Put another way, central government bureaucracies have not grown so quickly or obviously as have the number of "fringe bodies", including interest groups.[24]

Pre-Thatcherite influence of the environmental lobby

In the environmental arena, there is no question that voluntary groups are central to the policy process in Britain. Andy Wilson of CPRE argues that groups make policy in Britain: "they come up with the ideas and create the pressure – the civil servants just rewrite the ideas".[25] Where other industrialized countries may design and implement environmental policy through government agencies, many functions in Britain are carried out by private groups. This may be one reason why the British government has been so inactive on environmental issues. The National Trust, for example, does much more than the government in acquiring and maintaining historic buildings and scenic landscape. The Trust, the Royal Society for the Protection of Birds and county naturalists' trusts between them own and manage 756,000 acres of protected land. By contrast, state national nature reserves – managed by the Nature Conservancy Council – cover just 343,000 acres.

Despite its large numbers and its widespread support, the pre-Thatcherite influence of the environmental movement was limited at best. Writing in the early 1980s, Philip Lowe and Jane Goyder argued that although the movement was larger than either the consumer or the women's movements in the 1970s, it had won fewer institutional reforms. They felt that its political impact in the 1970s and early 1980s may have been eclipsed by the smaller and more vociferous anti-nuclear movement; "Perhaps the greatest failing of environmental groups in the 1970s was their inability to translate their massive numerical support into an appreciable political force."[26]

Tim O'Riordan reached similar conclusions, describing British environmental groups as "politically active but only sporadically influential". Any power they may have had, he argued, was a product of their respectability and campaigning credibility, and for the most part they had tended to take on the attire, reasoning and behaviour of the establishment; truly radical environmental opposition in Britain had steadily declined. Environmental politics in Britain was not radical in the sense that it promoted novel, visionary or unconventional ideas; it was "essentially reactive and accommodative to prevailing political realities. It is not the visionary politics of far-sighted ecological housekeeping."[27]

In the British system, direct political confrontation and disruptive techniques are rare. Among environmental groups, only Greenpeace has tended to use such techniques, although it has become less confrontational with time. Groups are also handicapped by their unequal access to the political system. Because they are not seen by government to be of central importance to the effective performance of government or the economy, they do not have the close, symbiotic relationship with senior civil servants in the central departments which corporate interest groups enjoy. This means they are not automatically included at the formative stages of policy-making, although they are usually consulted at a later stage.[28]

Until the 1970s, environmental groups relied mainly on private negotiations with government officials to influence the policy process. Lacking equal access, many later became more involved in direct lobbying, political activism and the mobilization of public opinion. Environmental groups in the early 1980s faced a mixed reception from policy-makers. In their 1983 study of groups, Philip Lowe and Jane Goyder found that government was not a passive recipient of pressure from environmental groups but "an active agent, establishing new consultative procedures, funding environmental groups, even promoting the creation of such groups".[29] They found that most groups were regularly in touch with government departments or public agencies, and that most had personal contacts. Members of both Houses of Parliament held official or honorary positions in many environmental organizations; many groups had government observers on their executive committees; and many were also represented on official advisory committees. Not all government departments or agencies were uniformly receptive, though;

the least receptive were development-oriented departments, such as those of energy, trade, industry and transport, and the CEGB.[30]

Influence was, however, a two-way street, and the government used several methods to limit the effectiveness of the environmental lobby. First, consultation is often seen as a privilege, not a right. British interest groups generally win and keep that privilege by adhering to an unwritten code of moderate and responsible behaviour. Consultation rights can be withdrawn if a group is too outspoken or fails to show the necessary tact and discretion. Groups drawn into consultation with departments or agencies have often been persuaded to moderate their demands and tactics.

Secondly, while many interest groups derive their political power from the fact that their co-operation is vital to the implementation of policy or the normal functioning of government, environmental groups generally did not have this power. Their only significant powers by the early 1980s were public censure and delay, and these were used sparingly and as a last resort, for fear of attracting counter-measures.

Thirdly, groups have always had to be careful not to become so overtly politically active as to lose their charitable status. Charitable groups are not allowed in principle to take part in overt political activities. Since more than half the environmental groups in Britain are charities, any lobbying they are involved in must be discreet and restrained. This means they dress up their media activities as public education rather than propaganda. Groups like Friends of the Earth have even set up separate charitable trusts to support their educational and research work. This lets the groups get on with their campaigning activities.

Fourthly, groups were pushed to the margin of decision-making. They were given most access to quangos such as the Countryside Commission and the Nature Conservancy Council, which had little money or power, and were politically marginal. In addition, these agencies themselves tended to be regarded by government as interest groups, "whose views should be treated with scepticism and whose involvement in central policy making should be carefully circumscribed".[31] This in turn encouraged the quangos to work at moderating the demands of groups, and to mediate between groups and the government.

Fifthly, groups were pushed towards local government. The effect of this was to concentrate environmental opposition at the local level, deflecting it away from the national policies of central government. Hence much environmental pressure was expended on challenging local development projects. Finally, groups were handicapped by the secretive nature of British government. Like all lobbies, the environmental lobby had to rely to a very large extent on leaks and whistle-blowing for its political effectiveness. The secrecy surrounding much of the British political process made it difficult for groups to work to change that process.

Conclusions

The environment has not to date been a prominent part of the British public policy agenda. Environmental policy is poorly understood and restrictively defined; the institutional and legislative response to environmental management has been piecemeal, confused and incomplete; and the sectors of British society that are the particular subject of environmental regulation have often had considerable influence on how those regulations are designed and implemented. Consultation between the regulators and the regulated, together with reliance on voluntary codes of compliance, has long been the basis of much environmental policy-making and implementation in Britain.

At the same time, much of the responsibility for environmental protection has been taken by a large and active voluntary sector. Despite this, the relative unimportance of the environment as a political issue has combined with the relatively limited influence of non-economic interest groups in the policy process to marginalize and restrict the influence of the environmental lobby. In fact, it is true to say that Britain simply does not have an environmental policy, nor (with the exception of the Greens) do individual British political parties. For these reasons, Britain has often lagged behind many other industrialized liberal democracies in recognizing and responding to environmental problems.

2. The Environmental Lobby

Politics and government in liberal democracies usually involve competition and compromise between different interests. Government departments, state-owned and private industries, professional associations, companies, business associations and local authorities may compete with each other to influence public policy, and try to exert pressure for change. Another group of organizations – interest groups – do the same, only more obviously.

There are many different definitions of interest groups, most of which differ in degree but not in substance. Jeffrey Berry's definition is the best and simplest: interest groups are organized bodies of individuals who share some goals and who try to influence public policy. They do this by lobbying, an activity which Berry believes includes "just about any legal means used to try to influence government".[1] He sees them as a primary link between citizens and government, a channel of access through which members voice their opinions to those who govern them.

Peter Madgwick argues that pressure groups differ from interest groups in that they have an interest to protect and foster, and an idea to promote, which interest groups do not. He argues that pressure groups "are to some extent incorporated in government, taking part in the processes of government, in consultation, advice and in some cases policy-making and implementation".[2]

S. E. Finer combines interest and pressure groups in a

"lobby", which he defines as "the sum of organizations in so far as they are occupied at any point of time in trying to influence the policy of public bodies in their own chosen direction; though (unlike political parties) never themselves prepared to undertake the direct government of the country".[3]

For present purposes, "interest" and "pressure" are taken to be two sides of the same coin. In Britain, there is an environmental "lobby" made up of individual environmental "interest groups". These are defined as non-governmental organizations (membership or non-membership) whose various methods and activities are wholly or mostly aimed at promoting rational and sustainable environmental management, through direct or indirect influence on public policy. (Excluded from this definition are private corporations, quangos, unions, industrial confederations, interest/pressure groups and any other organizations whose environmental interests are peripheral or subsidiary to their primary functions.)

The evolution of the environmental lobby

The modern British environmental movement is essentially a product of the last thirty years, but its origins go back much further. The foundations were arguably laid with the work of amateur field naturalists during the sixteenth, seventeenth and eighteenth centuries. Their work led to the development of modern botany, zoology and other life sciences.[4] With the help of lithography – invented in 1796–8 – the visual beauty of nature was made available to a wider public. All this combined with the findings of the age of British exploration to encourage research in the natural sciences, culminating in the theories of Darwin and Wallace. For a few at least, this was the beginning of a rediscovery of the place of the human race in nature.

With the improvement of transport in the nineteenth century, the countryside was made more accessible to the increasing number of Victorians seeking education, leisure, self-improvement and escape from the horrors of urban life. By the 1880s there were several hundred natural history societies and field clubs in Britain, with a combined membership of about 100,000.[5] Initially, these amateur naturalists were mainly interested in simply studying and enjoying nature, rather than preserving it. But as natural history and ornithology grew in popularity, specimen collecting became more common, and there was a corresponding growth in the damage inflicted on wild plants and animals. The preservation of nature now became implicit in the study of nature, and clubs and naturalists became concerned at the damage inflicted both by their own kind and by others. As naturalists learned more about nature, so they recognized its value and the scale of the threats posed by human activity.

Another early influence on the environmental movement came with growing concern about animal welfare. Hunting had long been a popular pastime, and few saw it as a cause for concern, but wanton slaughter and cruelty were different matters.[6] The same humanitarian zeal which had spawned the anti-slavery movement in the early nineteenth century also gave rise to a crusade against cruelty to animals. The Society for the Prevention of Cruelty to Animals (precursor to the RSPCA) was founded in 1824. Cruelty to animals was seen as an expression of the most savage and primitive elements in human nature. Protectionists believed that their efforts to save wildlife were contributing towards helping preserve the very fabric of society.[7]

Popular social reform movements often borrow techniques from one another, and attract support from the same quarters. The methods of Victorian abolitionists and those opposed to cruelty to animals now began to influence naturalists. A turning-point came in the 1860s when the protectionist crusade mustered its forces around the issue of the killing of birds to provide plumage for women's fashions.[8] The plumage issue was almost certainly the first popular protectionist cause, and was important in bringing protectionism closer to natural history.

The East Riding Association for the Protection of Sea Birds, founded in 1867 to campaign against the annual shoots of seabirds off Flamborough Head, may have been the first wildlife preservation body in the world.[9] The opposition to the killing of birds for plumage was led by women themselves, who made up the bulk of the membership of the earliest bodies. One of those was the Society for the Protection of Birds, founded in 1889 and given its royal charter in 1904. The SPB pledged its members not to wear plumage, and set up a network of national and overseas branches.

The reaction against development meanwhile hardened during the second half of the nineteenth century, when urban social conditions came under closer scrutiny. Revulsion at the squalor of life in industrial towns combined with the yearning for solace in open space and nature to produce the amenity movement. The world's first private environmental group was the Commons, Open Spaces and Footpaths Preservation Society, founded in 1865. The Society campaigned for the preservation of land for amenity, particularly the urban commons that were often the nearest "countryside" available to urban workers. Its pressure tactics succeeded, but it lacked corporate status and so could not buy land. This need was met in 1893 with the creation of the National Trust, which aimed to protect the nation's cultural and natural heritage from the standardization caused by industrial development.

The National Trust acquired land for preservation, but it was interested as much in sites of cultural and historic interest as it was in preserving nature. Naturalists began worrying about what they saw as the almost random way in which potential nature reserves were acquired, with apparently little regard for the national significance of their plants and animals.[10] In 1912 the Society for the Promotion of Nature Reserves (SPNR) was created, not to own nature reserves itself but to stimulate the National Trust to give due regard to the creation of reserves. (In 1981 the SPNR became the Royal Society for Nature Conservation.) Ironically, the National Trust was condemned by its own success in acquiring properties to expend more and more of its resources on land agency and management. This opened the way for the creation in 1926 of the Council for the Protection of Rural England (CPRE), founded to co-ordinate the voluntary movement, promote legislation and give advice to landowners.

By the inter-war years, then, Britain had a growing community of charitable bodies working to promote various aspects of nature protection. They focused on wildlife and countryside, a focus that was to remain an abiding interest of the British environmental movement. The American movement, by contrast, which emerged more or less coincidentally, was much more concerned with wildlife and wilderness preservation; that was the main goal of American groups like the Audubon Society (1889), the Sierra Club (1892) and the Wilderness Society (1935).

Although the foundations of British environmentalism were laid in the period 1860–1910, it was not until much later that the environmental lobby emerged as an appreciable force in British politics. As in many other industrialized countries, the 1960s saw a new awareness of environmental issues in Britain, prompted by several different events.

- Nuclear tests during the 1950s emphasized humanity's ability to pollute the global atmosphere, and to set off changes in the environment that no one really understood.
- The publication of Rachel Carson's *Silent Spring* (1962) made people aware for the first time of the dangers of man-made chemical fertilizers and pesticides in the environment.
- Advances in scientific understanding of natural processes made more people aware of the potential harm in human manipulation of the environment.
- Headline-catching environmental disasters such as the Aberfan disaster of 1966, and the *Torrey Canyon* disaster of 1967, gave environmental degradation a new and dramatic immediacy.
- A generation of scientists – dubbed the "prophets of doom" – spelled out the danger of population growth and misused technology.

This second wave of heightened environmental interest reached a peak in 1972 with the convening of the United

Nations Conference on the Human Environment in Stockholm. For the first time, governments sat down together to discuss the environment as a global policy issue. They debated the costs of unsustainable development, and they recognized for the first time the differing perceptions of rich and poor countries. In this receptive atmosphere, Britain – like most other liberal democracies – improved its body of environmental legislation, and strengthened its policy-making institutions. There were also changes among environmental interest groups.

First, existing groups attracted new support. Between 1967 and 1980, for example, membership of the Royal Society for the Protection of Birds rose from 38,000 to 321,000, and that of the National Trust (whose interests go beyond nature protection) from 159,000 to nearly a million. The number of local amenity societies increased sixfold between 1958 and 1975; by 1977 they had a total membership of 300,000.

Secondly, groups became less parochial and more aware of the international dimensions of many environmental issues. The World Wide Fund for Nature (WWF) was founded in Switzerland in 1961 (largely at the instigation of British environmentalists such as Max Nicholson and Peter Scott) to raise money for the conservation of wildlife. Until its recent name-change, undertaken to signify its broader interests, the Fund was called simply the World Wildlife Fund.

Finally, the interests of the movement broadened, reflecting a growing recognition that threats to wildlife and the countryside were only the symptoms of wider economic and social questions that needed to be addressed. The changed emphasis was reflected most notably in the creation of Friends of the Earth and Greenpeace, organizations very different from those that had come before. Friends of the Earth (FoE) was founded in the United States in 1969 and Greenpeace in Canada in 1972, both with the aim of using vigorous public campaigning to draw attention to broader threats to the environment. FoE was founded by David Brower, previously executive director of the Sierra Club, who had been removed from that post because his confrontational methods had led to the Sierra Club's loss of its tax-exempt status.[11]

Perhaps the most significant change in the course of the environmental movement came in the 1980s, with the emergence of green political parties arguing the need for a fundamental reordering of prevailing economic and political systems. Greens believe that neither capitalism nor socialism can deal efficiently with basic human demands, that society has become too big and impersonal and that people should see themselves as part of a wider environmental system, and understand more fully the consequences of human activity for that system.

Structure of the environmental lobby

Britain has the oldest, strongest, best-organized and most widely supported environmental lobby in the world. The last comprehensive survey of British environmental groups was undertaken in 1981–2 by Philip Lowe and Jane Goyder. They estimated the total membership of the movement at between 2.5 and 3 million members (4.5 to 5.3 per cent of the total population).[12] This made it the largest mass movement in British history. Between 1982 and 1990, there was more growth in support for environmental groups; by 1990, the membership of the British environmental movement probably stood closer to 4.5 million (or 8 per cent of the population).

Some environmental groups are transitory, either because they are created in response to time-specific or place-specific issues, or because they fall victim to poor management, lack of support and/or over-extension. This makes it difficult to be sure at any one time of the exact number of organizations that make up the environmental lobby. A 1990 directory lists more than 1,500 organizations "concerned in some way with the environment" in the British Isles.[13] Many of these are governmental or international bodies, bodies with very specialized interests, professional and trade associations, local offices of national groups, consultancies or peace organizations. Excluding these, the directory lists 65 non-governmental organizations working at the national level on aspects of environmental protection of general interest, 62 local groups (mainly county wildlife and naturalists' trusts) and 16 regional groups (restricted to Scotland, Wales and/or Northern Ireland).

The words "movement" and "lobby" imply homogeneity, co-operation, singleness of purpose, unity and steady evolution. But this is misleading. Observers of social and political movements have identified many different kinds of groups. There are sectional groups, with demands that can often be conceded with minimal public controversy.[14] There are economic and ideological groups.[15] There are functional groups (mainly pursuing economic interests) and preference groups ("united by common tastes, attitudes or pastimes").[16] There are emphasis groups, whose aims do not conflict in any clear-cut way with widely held social goals or values but which are motivated by a belief in the importance of certain values and the need for vigilance on their behalf (such as the National Trust), and promotional groups, which promote causes involving social or political reform (such as the Green Party).[17]

"The environment" is such a broad and far-reaching concept that environmental interest groups could be placed in many of these sub-categories. Certainly they promote a cause, and they also have economic and social interests. A number of groups also have sectional interests. One category which does *not* apply is ideology; many environmentalists argue that the environment is not an ideological issue, even though socialists, liberals and conservatives may have very different responses to the idea of environmental regulation and protection.

As with any other popular mass movement (for example, the women's movement, the peace movement and the civil rights movement), the environmental movement (globally and nationally) is made up of diverse, separate organizations, pursuing roughly the same goals but using different methods.

- Interests vary from the relatively narrow (such as the Royal Society for the Protection of Birds, the Campaign for Lead-Free Air, the Campaign Against Sea Dumping, the Soil Association and Men of the Trees) to the relatively broad (the National Trust, the World Wide Fund for Nature, Friends of the Earth, and so on).

- Some groups focus on a specific domain, such as the countryside (Council for the Protection of Rural England), public awareness (Television Trust for the Environment), wildlife preservation (People's Trust for Endangered Species), air pollution (National Society for Clean Air), energy conservation (Association for the Conservation of Energy, Centre for Alternative Technology), hunting (British Association for Shooting and Conservation), ideological interests (Socialist Environment and Resources Association, Green Democrats), transport (Transport 2000), education (Council for Environmental Education), professional interests (Association of Conservation Officers) and amenity and recreation (Ramblers'Association, Open Spaces Society).
- The methods and tactics of groups include overt lobbying (Friends of the Earth, Green Alliance), research (Earth Resources Research), field studies (Field Studies Council), practical voluntary work (British Trust for Conservation Volunteers), fund-raising and public education (National Trust, World Wide Fund for Nature) and providing consultancy services to industry (SustainAbility, Conservation Foundation).
- The size and wealth of groups vary enormously. The National Trust is by far the largest, with a membership of 1.75 million, and an income in 1989 of £55.8 million. The median income for groups is considerably less – probably in the vicinity of £100,000 per year. Membership figures can be as low as a few hundred.
- Most groups are voluntary organizations and registered charities with open membership; some have restricted membership or no membership (Institute for European Environmental Policy); others are limited companies (Environmental Data Services, Environmental Resources Ltd); others are trade associations (British Waste Paper Association).

Few of these groups work in a vacuum; most are in touch with many other groups. There are so many groups, and so many issues, that continuing liaison would be a complex matter. Hence most co-ordination tends to be *ad hoc* and informal, rather than structured and ongoing. It may consist of the creation of coalitions to deal with specific issues, the presentation of joint manifestos and statements or, most commonly, unstructured personal contacts; the staff of most groups tend to know their counterparts in other groups and to maintain regular contact. Most groups exchange literature and information, and some even share staff and offices (for example, the International Institute for Environment and Development shares its London offices with at least seven other groups). All groups consider themselves part of a wider environmental movement.

Jonathon Porritt believes that groups have a pragmatic, flexible approach to co-operation:

> If any legislative initiative gets under way which will involve different groups, they will get together to determine tactics. This approach developed at the time of the Wildlife and Countryside Act, when all the groups worked out what they wanted to say and how they would approach the same target differently. Each used different tactics, but knew why the others were using *their* tactics.[18]

The formal arrangements for co-ordination are fragmentary. The Council for Environmental Conservation (CoEnCo) was founded in 1969 to co-ordinate the work of the environmental lobby. For a variety of reasons (some relating to internal organizational and personnel problems, and others to wider external factors, such as the unwillingness of individual groups to give up authority to umbrella organizations), CoEnCo had all but ceased to exist by the mid-1980s. Since renamed the Environment Council, it now restricts most of its activities to its wildlife committee, Wildlife Link, which is a liaison body primarily involved in information exchange. With three full-time staff and forty-three member organizations, Wildlife Link cannot make statements on behalf of other groups. It works mainly with the Department of the Environment and the Ministry of Agriculture, Fisheries and Food and is particularly useful for smaller groups which lack significant political contacts of their own.[19] In addition to Wildlife Link, there is a group called Countryside Link which acts as a forum for meetings between groups and the Countryside Commission, and there are separate co-ordinating groups for Scotland (Scottish Wildlife and Countryside Link) and Northern Ireland (Northern Ireland Environmental Link).

The second co-ordinating group is the Green Alliance, founded in 1978 to improve the parliamentary intelligence and strategy of the environmental lobby. It concentrates on agenda-setting, on encouraging other institutions (in government and industry) to give more attention to environmental policy issues and on helping groups better understand the nature of the political process. As the director of the Green Alliance, Tom Burke, puts it: "We want to help groups distinguish between the political process (what many people do at many levels) and the governmental process (what a small number of people do). If you want to change the agenda you have to understand politics."[20]

Environmental groups and the policy process

Public policy is not simply made by an elected government; it is often made outside formal governing structures, frequently by non-elected and non-accountable officials and individuals. Jordan and Richardson argue that the simple model of a political system as a process by which an electorate chooses a government, which then presents a coherent set of policies based on a party's election manifesto for parliamentary approval, misses much of the variety and complexity of how political decisions are made. They see political activity as conducted largely in "policy communities" of interested groups and government departments and agencies.[21] They approach the assessment of policy-making in Britain by dividing it into six arenas: the public arena, Parliament, parties, the cabinet, the bureaucratic arena and the interest group arena. Other assessments of policy-making include "arenas" as diverse as corporations, courts (where appropriate) and the media. As far as British environmental groups are concerned, there are five main arenas of interest: government departments, political parties, Parliament, the public arena and the international arena.

Government departments

The prime minister and cabinet may be the government, but there are few people who see the cabinet as a really substantial policy-making body. For Richard Crossman, it was "not a coherent effective policy-making body; it is a collection of departmental Ministers".[22] Lord Butler recalls how most of his work as Minister of Education "was done outside the Cabinet and I hardly referred to the Cabinet at all".[23] The MacDonald cabinet was apparently one where "only routine daily business was transacted – very few big questions of policy were discussed".[24]

Britain has been increasingly governed along prime ministerial lines, which means that cabinet ministers (especially in the Thatcher administration) have been mainly interested in preserving their positions in the cabinet. On the one hand, they feel obliged to maintain the unwritten rule of collective responsibility, and to put this above their own individual goals and values. On the other hand, they also feel obligated to the needs of their departments, and rely heavily on the advice and support of their senior civil servants. Although ministers in theory have absolute power over policy formulation and the work of their departments, they usually have less real power and influence than their senior civil servants.[25] There are several reasons for this.

First, ministers are overburdened and busy, and have to rely on their officials for the information they need to make decisions. Secondly, officials have access to an informal network of officials in different departments. If their own minister rejects their advice, they can enlist the support of officials in other departments, who may encourage *their* ministers to overrule or persuade the first minister against his decision. Finally, ministers are not allowed to see the papers of previous administrations. This puts them at a disadvantage when compared with their officials, who have the advantage of continuity and greater familiarity with past procedures and decisions.

For these reasons, environmental groups – like most other interest groups – have found the cabinet of little interest and value, but have found individual departments and their staff more useful. The relationship between environmental groups and departments has improved markedly in recent years, mainly as a result of the relative decline of influence of economic interest groups, the growing prominence of the environment as a policy issue, and strengthened environmental regulation arising from changes in the structure of government. The farming lobby is not as powerful as it was ten years ago (see Chapter 4); the water and electricity supply industries have been privatized and their regulatory activities given to new independent organizations; and the European Community has begun to bring about a fundamental change in the nature of regulation and environmental policy-making in Britain. All of this has helped the environmentalists.

Parties

British political parties have played only a marginal role in the environmental debate. None except the Greens have a comprehensive environmental policy, and the environment tends to be a minor issue in election manifestos. The 1987 Conservative manifesto mentioned the environment only as part of a basket of miscellaneous issues bundled together under the headline "A Better Society". The manifestos of all three major parties in 1987 outlined piecemeal environmental programmes, making general references to issues such as nuclear power, pollution control, energy conservation and green belt protection.

Given the obvious dissatisfaction among environmentalists with Conservative policy during the 1980s, opposition parties might have used the opportunity to offer more constructive and well-considered alternative policies, but they did not. The Social Democrats convened an environmental policy group in 1982 to prepare for the next election, but it was poorly led and was able to offer little more than a proposal for a reorganization of government machinery. It was clearly a missed opportunity. Porritt believes that Mrs Thatcher's 1988 statements on the environment caught the opposition parties unaware. "They flirted with going green without actually doing it," he argues. "Labour saw the environment as too middle class an issue. Thatcher's speech created the agenda for green issues, a fact which the opposition deeply regrets."[26]

Labour has the oldest party environmental group: the Socialist Environment and Resources Association, founded in 1973. SERA now describes itself as "the green wing of the Labour movement and the socialist wing of the green movement".[27] In 1988, the Green Democrats were founded to replace the Liberal Ecology Group, and the Tory Green Initiative was created to "campaign for an environmentally sensitive free-market economy . . . and to communicate Government achievements and future plans to a wider public audience".[28]

There are some who argue that parties as organizations are in a state of decline in Britain, due partly to disappointment with party performance while in office, and partly to the growing popularity of new styles of political participation.[29] The inexorable rise of interest groups in Britain has contributed to the decline of parties as key organizations in the political system.[30] It is arguable that interest groups are a more accurate (if not always more efficient) way of representing citizen interests than political parties.

For environmental groups, political parties have been of only slightly more interest than the cabinet. In 1982, Lowe and Goyder found a general lack of interest among groups in parties; few groups made any real effort to influence party policies, due to a feeling that governments did not feel bound to party manifestos, and to a feeling that most environmental issues anyway transcended party politics.[31] Interest groups generally tend to avoid too close an association with a particular party for the same reasons. The staff of groups interviewed for this study expressed similar views. Little or no mention was made of contacts with party organizations.

The level of party interest in the environment may have begun to change since 1988–9. Green Party successes at local and European parliamentary elections in May and June 1989 raised once again the theoretical possibility of a change in the make-up of the British political party spectrum; at the very least, it focused the minds of Conservative, Labour and Liberal Democratic party strategists more clearly on environmental issues. In August 1989, the Labour Party announced the formation of a new campaign unit charged with reorganizing Labour environmental policy. This followed the publication of an internal party report suggesting that environmentalism was now a permanent electoral phenomenon, which Labour was best placed to handle. Among other things, the party planned to create an informal network of contacts with interest groups working on environmental, countryside and energy issues.

Nigel Haigh believes that the 1989 European elections had an important effect on raising party awareness of environmental issues, a process that has since been further promoted by environmental groups. Three years before, he observes, the average MP could make a speech about housing, Northern Ireland or defence off the top of his or her head, but they could not make a speech on the environment.

> The Euro elections had a dramatic effect. Suddenly ordinary MPs were beginning to bone up on the environment, and that's where the [groups] came in. MPs wanted information, and talked to their local environmental groups to get that information. They clearly wanted to know.[32]

Parliament

Most political scientists agree that Parliament is the least important or influential arena of policy-making in Britain. If the government has a majority, and as long as it can keep that majority intact, the government will control Parliament. Most successful amendments to bills tend to be moved by government ministers themselves; government backbenchers and the opposition tend to have very little input into the final outcome of most bills. Ministers present to Parliament a package already agreed between civil servants and interest groups, and backbenchers are generally loath to challenge the government and party discipline.

The only time that Parliament can really assert itself is when the government has a precarious majority, or when a major public or political issue arises where a considerable amount of work has to be done to persuade large numbers of MPs or peers to oppose or change government policy. Charles Miller suggests that MPs are increasingly resentful of modern lobbying, for two reasons: first, much lobbying directed at MPs should be directed rather at Whitehall; and second, the techniques of modern lobbyists are sufficiently disembodied that MPs are often approached as a mass audience, even though their interests may not coincide with those of the lobbyists.[33] He believes that the real effectiveness of MPs now lies in their role as guardians of constituency interests, and as extra-parliamentary negotiators with ministers. Individual MPs have readier access to ministers than do members of the public, and can make private representations to ministers.

Environmental groups have had generally productive and active relations with Parliament. Out of 74 groups surveyed by Lowe and Goyder in 1981–2, 62 said they could count on the assistance of at least one MP or peer (the median was 9 MPs per group). Of those groups, 19 had regular contact with more than thirty MPs or peers, and most had parliamentary agents or links with all-party groups of backbenchers and peers (such as the Conservation Committee and the Ecology Group). The House of Lords is particularly useful to groups. Peers have fewer commitments than MPs, and can become involved in the work of groups. Many hereditary peers are large landowners with personal interests in rural conservation. Party links and discipline are also weaker in the Lords.[34] By contrast, MPs have proved less effective. Jonathon Porritt describes Conservative backbenchers as "mindless lobby fodder", noting their obvious unwillingness to revolt against their leaders.[35]

Alistair Gammell of the RSPB suggests three possible reasons for the low interest shown by MPs in the environment. First, their own professional backgrounds as teachers, lawyers, and so on, makes MPs less likely to show an interest in the environment. Secondly, with voters knowing and caring relatively little about the environment until recently, they do not approach their MPs on environmental issues. Gammell himself ran for Parliament in 1983, and recalls receiving no questions at all on the environment. Finally, there is the influence of party discipline in the House of Commons. It is because peers are less beholden to whips in the House of Lords that nearly all the amendments to legislation achieved by environmental groups have been won in the Lords.[36]

In terms of the sheer volume of activity involving groups and Parliament, Jordan and Richardson suggest that it sometimes seems as though there is much group activity at the parliamentary level; however, the link between "noise" and real influence is weak.[37] Only once has there been a substantial group role in influencing the activities of Parliament on an environmental issue; this occurred in 1970 with the success of the Wing group in engineering the formation of an all-party committee to co-ordinate opposition to a third London airport. At other times, though, groups and peers in particular have worked closely to amend legislation, notably the 1981 Wildlife and Countryside Act.

Where co-operation exists, parliamentarians offer groups help on legislation (through the introduction of amendments, or opposition to parts of private bills), enlisting the support of colleagues, sponsoring legislation, acting as spokespeople, encouraging parliamentary select committees to take up issues, inviting interested groups to give evidence to committees, providing information and parliamentary intelligence and providing links to ministers. Groups in return offer expertise in the drafting of bills.

The public arena

Public debate is a central part of democracy. Government policies are often judged and accepted or rejected on the basis of their electoral impact. However, politicians often disregard the wishes of voters if their conscience, ideology or relationship with powerful interest groups presses them to ignore public opinion.[38] This has certainly been the case with environmental issues, where opinion polls have consistently shown high public support for new policy initiatives, but the Thatcher administration was slow to respond.

Of all the policy arenas, environmental groups have been

most active (and have had the most success) in the public arena. Despite – or perhaps because of – Thatcherism; and perhaps thanks in part to their relatively limited access to the other arenas of policy-making, environmental groups have worked actively to create an environmentally conscious electorate. They have done this most notably through contacts with the media, which proved consistently successful throughout the 1970s and 1980s. Most groups had extensive media contacts and won growing coverage in the press, on radio and on TV, in that order. Lowe and Goyder noted a growth in the use of the media during the 1960s and 1970s. They felt there had been a deliberate strategy on the part of groups to promote "open" politics, and that it was not simply the last resort of groups otherwise excluded from private consultation. Groups came to depend less on personal influence and behind-the-scenes string-pulling, and more on an open adversarial approach, and direct appeals to popular opinion.[39]

There are repeated examples of successful or influential campaigns being run by environmental groups through the media, aimed at changing either policy or public opinion. During the 1970s, groups generated public concern over the issues of heavy trucks, cyanide dumping and the demolition of particular historic buildings. More recently, the Campaign for Lead-Free Air (CLEAR) orchestrated a media campaign against lead in fuel during the early 1980s, which contributed to raising public awareness, which in turn helped lead in 1989 to the introduction of subsidized lead-free petrol throughout Britain (see Chapter 7).

The international arena

An influence often overlooked in studies of policy-making is that of foreign governments and international organizations on domestic politics. With the growing interdependence of global political and economic systems, national governments are experiencing an increase in the number of policy decisions that can only be taken with reference to other governments. There was a notable globalization of environmental issues during the 1980s, and groups found themselves working with non-British groups and government agencies on issues such as acid pollution, threats to the ozone layer, marine pollution and global warming. They also found themselves working increasingly through international fora to change domestic policy. British groups have long played an active role, for example, in the European Environmental Bureau (which liaises with the European Community) and the Environment Liaison Centre, a Nairobi-based organization which oversees liasion between non-governmental groups and the UN Environment Programme (UNEP). Most importantly, groups have found that the European Community has opened up an important and influential channel through which domestic British policy can be formed and amended (see Chapter 7).

Conclusions

The environmental movement in Britain is large, active and well-supported, and rests on a tradition of public and private interest in the condition of the environment that has grown and widened over the past 150 years. Environmental groups are many and varied, using different tactics to achieve different but largely complementary objectives.

However, the level of access of environmental groups to government departments, political parties and Parliament has been variable. Although most groups have long had good and regular contacts with ministers, government departments and backbenchers, as of the early 1980s the movement had not been able to translate its numerical power into appreciable and consistent direct political influence of the kind enjoyed by economic interests and lobbies, such as the agriculture and business lobbies.

With some exceptions, the most substantial achievements of the environmental lobby have occurred either through practical activities such as species and habitat protection, or through indirect influence on policy-makers through careful and increasingly professional use of the public arena. Probably the most lasting impact of the lobby during the 1970s and 1980s came through the work it did to promote public awareness of environmental issues. The result was that it was able to bring about changes in public attitudes despite the relatively low level of interest in environmental management within government.

3. Thatcherism and the Environment

Alone among twentieth-century prime ministers, Margaret Thatcher's name has been applied to a set of political ideas and a style of administration. Winning power at a time when Britain had been experiencing persistent economic decline and political disfunction, Thatcher believed she had identified the key elements of the "British disease", and set out to give Britain the hard medicine that she believed had to be applied if the decline was to be reversed. Above all, she felt, this meant an end to consensus, an abandonment of the agreement and continuity between socialist and conservative governments on the mixed economy and the welfare state. It also meant putting an end to compromise, bargaining and the search for policies acceptable to the majority. In its place, Mrs Thatcher wanted a new kind of politics, variously labelled adversarial, confrontational or conviction politics.

The "British disease" has been described in many different ways. At one time or another, though, all the following elements have appeared in those descriptions:

- An overdependence on interest groups and consultation as a method of governance. Most notably, conservatives felt that trade unions had become too powerful, leading to the repeated reliance of governments on consultation with – and appeasement of – the unions, the use of strikes as a first resort and the loss of an increasing number of working days through industrial disputes.

- A welfare system that was proving expensive and was – to its critics – making too many people dependent upon the state, thereby reducing self-reliance and incentives for self-improvement, and contributing to economic decline.
- A declining position in world trade. Britain's share of world export trade fell from more than 25 per cent in 1950 to about 9 per cent between 1973 and 1977.
- A relative decline in productivity. Productivity during the 1950s and 1960s had grown at 3.1 per cent annually, compared to annual average rates of 5.6 per cent in West Germany, France and Italy; by 1973, the rate had fallen to just 0.2 per cent, compared to 3.8 per cent in France and 2.5 per cent in West Germany.
- A declining trade surplus. From a point in 1963 where Britain exported twice as much as it imported, its trade surplus had almost disappeared by the early 1970s.
- An industrial sector that was riven by class divisions and poor management.
- Little incentive for technological innovation, and a failure to apply technological innovation to industry.
- For Thatcher in particular, Britain's decline contained within it elements of social and moral decline. This was reflected in the rise of a counterculture, a conspiracy to rebel, a weakening of "family values", an increase in the incidence of crime and the compromising of "traditional" notions of law and order.

If Thatcherite policies had a consistent focus during the 1980s (and there is some debate about this), then it was the eradication of the British disease. Thatcherism came to be associated with "conviction politics": a rejection of consensus, and a belief in the guidance of one's own passionately held beliefs. Thatcherism was associated with markets, monetarism and authoritative government, and Thatcherite policies were aimed at producing a strong state and a free economy.[1] David Marquand argues that Thatcherism has four basic dimensions: "a sort of British Gaullism" born out of a growing sense of despair with Britain's decline; economic liberalism (a rejection both of macro-economic Keynesianism and of micro-economic intervention by public authorities); traditional Toryism (including patriotism and a pride in tradition); and a style of politics both populist and charismatic.[2]

If Thatcherism is classified as an ideology, then it has several basic arguments:

- The rolling back of the state.
- The promotion of an enterprise culture through the reduction of the public sector; the encouragement of a free market-oriented economy; and the reduction of subsidies so that businesses can find their true economic level. This has included the reduction or removal of government regulations on business, and the privatization of many previously state-owned industries and services, such as British Telecom, Jaguar, British Airways, the British Airports Authority and council housing.
- A freeing of the labour market through the curbing of trade union power, and the introduction of trade union reforms.
- The use of monetarist economic policies aimed at reducing the increase in money supply so as to reduce inflation, and cutting government expenditure so as to reduce public borrowing and income taxation. The reduction of taxes is in turn intended to promote savings, investment and entrepreneurial activity.
- Restoration of the authority of government through the strengthening of military defence and law and order, and through resisting the claims of interest groups.[3]
- The promotion of law and order and family values in order to promote a "higher" moral level in society.
- The restoration of Britain's position in the world, and the belief in strong British policy on supra-national issues, such as the European Community, the Western Alliance and, more recently, global environmental issues.

There is some debate about the extent to which Thatcherism can really be seen as an ideology rather than simply a style of government. Martin Holmes sees Thatcherism as "a relentless and determined pursuit of ideological goals";[4] but others describe Mrs Thatcher as an "entrepreneurial politician". Rather than having set out in 1979 with a clearly defined programme, it often seemed in the 1980s as though Mrs Thatcher developed policies instinctively, and took advantage of opportunities as they presented themselves.

Peter Jenkins argues that Thatcherism was more a style than an ideology, because it was instinctive rather than consistent or structured.[5] Philip Lowe suggests that critics of the left gave Thatcherism a philosophical coherence that it lacked. "Thatcherism [was] a radical stance to the economy," he argues,

> but it [was] much more a gut reaction than a well worked-out political philosophy. It is difficult to list its basic tenets. Thatcherism has been all about taking a sledgehammer to a whole set of social and economic relationships. It is radicalism verging on destructiveness. It's all about breaking up established, cosy relationships in government. It has been a catalyst for some environmental debates by allowing cosy procedures to be subjected to wider view.[6]

Privatization is a good example of the opportunistic (or pragmatic) nature of Thatcherism. Before 1979, the thinking of the Conservatives in opposition about privatization had been mainly negative – that is, what to do with the problem of nationalized industries. The 1979 election manifesto made only minor mention of the issue, and promised only the sale back to the private sector of the recently nationalized aerospace and shipbuilding industries, together with the sale of shares in other sectors. "As with so many other policies since 1979," notes Peter Riddell, "it was the experience, and the frustrations of office, which produced a more radical approach."[7]. Privatization did not move into high gear until the second Thatcher administration.

By its own admission, the government handled the privatization of water and electricity badly (see Chapter 5). Among other things, privatization unexpectedly raised new environmental issues to which the administration had to respond. Lowe argues that without the privatization of the water industry, the entire debate about the implementation of the European Community directive on drinking water would not have been advanced. Privatization subjected the water industry to close scrutiny, made water pollution a major public issue during 1989 and resulted in the creation of a new independent water pollution control agency. "This was a prime example of Thatcher breaking up established procedures so everyone could look inside," he argues.[8]

Thatcherism also involved a new style of administration. Anthony King argues that Thatcher proved an unusual prime minister in at least two respects. First, she was always a minority inside her own party and her own government in that she held very strong views, particularly on economic policy. Not many Tories fully shared her monetarist convictions, nor her single-minded belief that Britain had to face up to some "hard medicine". Secondly, unlike most prime ministers, she adopted a policy agenda that was peculiarly her own. She felt strongly about the substance of policy, and had policy aims in a large number of fields. King argues that she always had a clear, personal sense of direction, and was not just the Tory Party writ large. She was "more concerned with arriving at the right outcome than with how that outcome is reached".[9]

Part of the reason why so few prime ministers have had dictinct policy platforms is because the preferences of most prime ministers have traditionally been those of the party and the cabinet. King argues that British prime ministers are not generally in the position of having a large number of aims: "acts of genuine leadership, in which prime ministers try to steer their cabinets in directions in which they might not otherwise go, stand out precisely because of their comparative rarity".[10] Most prime ministers cannot make their own decisions because they have to carry their cabinets with them. Because there is no security of tenure, it is essential to keep the support of the cabinet. Most prime ministers do not take policy initiatives without first being sure they can count on the backing of their colleagues.[11]

This was never the case with Margaret Thatcher. Hugo Young has described her management style as that of the chairman who invariably leads from the front.[12] Simon Jenkins noted early in her administration that she had the reputation of "she who must be persuaded".[13] Initially in a minority in her cabinet, she proved assertive, often thought aloud, more often than not dominated cabinet meetings and was often defeated in cabinet.[14] Her assertive style stood in contrast to the styles of Wilson, Heath and Callaghan, who preferred "silently listening to the voices before exercising the prerogative of summing up".[15] Despite this, King argues that she was not destructively confrontational. "She is someone who prefers to fight another day, who is always ready to compromise."[16]

Unlike Edward Heath, Thatcher did not tend to respond to policy problems in organizational terms (by creating a new committee, or merging two departments). She was more people-centred, and thought in terms of the individuals who would be best at dealing with new problems and situations as they arose.[17] She was unconcerned with the structure of government. Her revolution, argues Martin Holmes, "has always been one of attitudes and policies as opposed to 1960s notions of institutional (or constitutional) change".[18] Preferring face-to-face argument and persuasion, she was her own chief of staff. She was determined to direct rather than merely to supervise,[19] and became closely involved in detailed decision-making. She was not seen in Whitehall as a remote figure. "Her presence is all-pervasive," notes King.[20]

Another characteristic of the office of the British prime minister is that there are few decisions prime ministers can take on their own authority; there are few statutes to administer, and – unlike the French or American presidents – the British prime minister has no department of his or her own. Yet one of the great strengths of the office is the fact that the outer limits of authority are so ill-defined. A determined prime minister can take more and more decisions. Throughout the 1980s, Thatcher extended her influence to senior civil service appointments, by working through small groups of ministers rather than the cabinet or cabinet committees, and by making clear to colleagues that she expected to be consulted at every stage in the policy process.[21]

Thatcherism, consensus and interest groups

Thatcherism is often associated with a rejection of consensus politics, but not everyone agrees that there was a consensus tradition before Mrs Thatcher came to power. "There never *was* a consensus," said Edward Heath in 1971. "The parties never came together in their policies. Even the idea of "Butskellism" was sloppy and inaccurate."[22] Peter Jenkins believes that consensus was founded more in myth than in reality. "Indeed, Britain suffered unduly . . . from sharp and usually ideologically inspired changes in direction."[23] Martin Holmes contends that

> the post-war consensus existed largely in name only from 1945 to 1972 . . . [It] was really tried, and pushed to its logical conclusions with zeal, only after the 1972 Heath U-turns. Its effects in all areas were negative and damaging; its deliverance came first from Jim Callaghan in 1976 and then from Margaret Thatcher after 1979.[24]

He goes on to suggest that while there was a Thatcherite attack on postwar consensus, the real target of Thatcherism was the failures of Conservative policy under the Heath administration.

Others believe that there *was* a consensus in British politics from about 1945 to about 1979; for them, the question was whether the consensus ended during the 1980s, and, if it had, what had Mrs Thatcher's role been in the process? Jordan and Richardson do not see the death of consensus, and reject Thatcher's claims of having changed the political landscape.[25] As evidence, they suggest that the opposition may argue against government policy, but does not promise to change it; that the government passes bills in some areas (after consultation with affected interests) which the opposition would have been obliged to introduce in roughly the same form; and that governments are themselves sometimes forced to reverse their own policies.[26] Jordan and Richardson quote Richard Rose's study of parties to support their conclusions. Rose shows that, during 1970–79, consensual behaviour was four times more likely than adversarial behaviour in Parliament.[27] (He says nothing, however, about changes in behaviour after 1979.)

Some observers feel that the consensus had already crumbled before Mrs Thatcher took power; David Butler and Dennis Kavanagh attribute this to widespread "disillusion with trade unions and parts of the public sector, and a sense of the failure of Keynesianism. . . . [What] was distinctive about Mrs Thatcher was that she was the first leader who did not try to make the consensus work."[28] Elsewhere, Kavanagh notes that a consensus prevailed in the 1950s and 1960s, and gradually broke down in the 1970s, but that it was "difficult to assign with precision responsibility for the breakdown of the consensus, though Mrs Thatcher wanted to break it and could claim some credit for doing so."[29] Some argue that monetarist policies were introduced by James Callaghan; for David Marquand, "the first monetarist Chancellor of the Exchequer since the war . . . was Denis Healey, not Geoffrey Howe".[30] Robert Skidelsky argues that trade union reform had been attempted well before Thatcher came to power, that the sale of council houses had been seriously considered by Wilson and Callaghan and that Callaghan had begun the debate on the quality of education.[31]

Others are more forthright in crediting Thatcher with a "revolution". S. E. Finer, for example, feels that Thatcherism marked a radical departure of an ideological kind because of the contrast with pre-1979 Keynesianism. He argues that Thatcherism "introduced a wholly new economic theory and practice and pursued them with obduracy and consistency".[32]

Whatever the disagreements on the existence of consensus politics, or Thatcher's relationship with the consensus approach, one thing is clear: Margaret Thatcher herself had no doubts about the existence of the consensus tradition. She believed that much of the blame for Britain's dilemma lay with consensus politics, a theme she pushed up to and beyond 1967, when she first won a place in the shadow cabinet. In an interview with the *Observer* before coming to power, Thatcher noted that her government "must be a conviction government. As Prime Minister I could not waste time having any internal arguments."[33] In 1981, she said: "For me, consensus seems to be the process of abandoning all beliefs, principles, values and policies";[34] it meant the appeasement of socialism and the advance of collectivism.[35] In a conversation in 1979 with Sir Anthony Parsons, then Ambassador to Iran, Thatcher was quoted as describing those who believed in consensus politics as "Quislings and traitors".[36]

For her critics on the left, Thatcher's disdain for consensus was seen as profoundly undemocratic, and suggested a dangerous tendency towards dictatorial government. Marxist analysts have seen Thatcherism as uncaring, as waging a war on "antisocial" groups such as feminists and gays (and on ethnic minorities), and as a form of social control. In the context of patriotism and the Falklands War, Tony Benn described Thatcherism as fascism. At the time of the 1984–5 coal-miners' strike, Arthur Scargill spoke of a class war between the forces of Thatcherism and the working class.

For Thatcher, consensus helped explain the apparent weakness of the Heath government; Heath's abandonment of his pledge to roll back the power of state had made him seem to his critics to be feeble and vacillating.[37] Peter Jenkins notes how Thatcherism was founded partly in the theory of a betrayal of principles, as exemplified by the decision of the Heath government in November 1972 to introduce statutory powers to control pay, prices and profits. This, combined with the reflationist policies of the Heath government, represented for Thatcher a continuation of the "disastrous collaboration with Keynesian consensus" which underlay so many of Britain's postwar economic problems.[38] The dramatic Conservative loss in 1974 had made Thatcher determined (when she took over the leadership of the Conservative Party) that in future there would be no U-turns.

Consensus means – among other things – consultation with interests, incremental change and the ability of interest groups to veto change. Samuel Beer has a particular dislike for consensus, arguing that consultation had led, by the 1960s, to stagnation and inertia.[39] In *Britain Against Itself*, Beer argued that British politics had been collectivized to the point where organized groups were the sole effective political actors.[40] For

Chapman in 1962, consensus policy-making meant finding "the least controversial course between the conflicting interests of vociferous private groups. It is not the doctrine of government: it is the doctrine of subordination."

For Mrs Thatcher, consensus too often meant appeasing interest groups and avoiding tough decisions. Nowhere was this more obvious (for her) than in the way in which postwar governments came to rely on reference to trade unions in designing and implementing policy. By the 1970s, the trade union question had become central to almost all economic policy debates. In 1984, Thatcher made a speech to the 1922 Committee including a now famous reference to the Scargill faction of the National Union of Mineworkers as "the enemy within".

One of the consistent themes of Thatcherism was the priority given to building a government strong enough to resist the influence of interest groups. (Mrs Thatcher was never opposed to *all* interest groups, only to those espousing policies that disagreed with her own. One of the paradoxes of Thatcherism was the obvious willingness to allow much more access to groups representing the management of business and industry than to those representing labour.)

Some of her ministers had similar thoughts on interest groups. In 1986, Douglas Hurd, then Home Secretary, warned of the growth of interest groups generally, likening them to "serpents emerging from the sea to strangle Laocoön and his sons in their coils". He feared that new legislation promoting freedom of information would allow interest groups to exert more pressure on government. Nicholas Ridley, while environment secretary, occasionally referred to environmental groups as "extremists" and "pseudo-Marxists". In July 1989, soon after the unexpectedly high vote for the Green Party at the European Parliament elections, Ridley spoke of environmental groups promoting "disinformation and wild accusations", and described the Green Party manifesto as "unscientific rubbish based on myths".

Thatcherism and the environment

Particularly since the late 1980s, there has been a relative flood of new studies of Thatcher and Thatcherism. Her policies and ideology have been subjected to close scrutiny and extensive discussion and analysis. In all this, the environment is barely mentioned, and where it is, it is usually in the context of Thatcherite performance on housing and local government. This is at least partly explained by the fact that, until 1988, the environment had barely even occurred to Mrs Thatcher as a significant policy issue. Environmentalists still remember a statement made by the Prime Minister during an address to the annual conference of the Scottish Conservative Party in May 1982. Speaking at the height of the Falklands War, she said: "When you've spent half your political life dealing with humdrum issues like the environment, it's exciting to have a real crisis on your hands."[41] Tom Burke believes that this unguarded comment was closer to her real beliefs about the environment than any actions she may have taken after 1988 suggesting growing sympathy for environmental issues.[42]

The relationship between Thatcherism and environmental policy can be divided into two phases: before and after September 1988. Before that date, Mrs Thatcher had consistently proven herself unsympathetic (at least in the public arena) to the goals and demands of environmental interest groups, or to the broader principles of environmentalism. For example, little was done during her first two administrations to reform or amend the administration of environmental management. The inadequacies of the Department of the "Environment" remained unaltered, and were aggravated by the appointment of secretaries of state with limited interest in the environment (with the possible exception of Michael Heseltine). For the environmental lobby, the nadir came with the appointment as environment secretary of Nicholas Ridley, a man almost universally condemned by environmental groups as having no environmental sympathies or understanding. Groups quoted the fact that Ridley was the only senior environmental minister in the European Community never to have attended any of the biannual meetings of the EC Council of Environment Ministers. Just before being removed from the department in July 1989, he proposed the creation of an independent environmental statistical office designed to counter what he felt was the "disinformation" provided by environmental interest groups.

The basic principles of environmental regulation and protection are built on values that are inherently antipathetic to the nature of Thatcherism. Many environmentalists argue that environmental protection demands regulation. Because resources such as the air and the oceans are in the public domain, they need protection against short-term, opportunistic exploitation (for example, as a ready conduit for the "free" disposal of pollutive and toxic wastes). Similarly, laws aimed at preventing rather than curing pollution demand up-front and often expensive investment in pollution-control equipment. The "polluter pays principle" is based on the argument that the polluting industry should meet the cost of pollution control, rather than dissipating the cost to society by polluting air and water. Many economists have long argued that the short-term profit motive is not the best approach to long-term environmental management.

However, the Thatcherite "enterprise culture" is based on ideas like voluntarism, self-regulation, competition and small government (including reduced government control of business and industry). Mrs Thatcher also set out to cut public spending in order to reduce taxation. The first two Thatcher administrations agreed to little (if any) investment in environmental management systems, greater reliance on the free market to promote such management and only minimal institutional reform. The only exception to the latter was the creation in 1987 of Her Majesty's Inspectorate of Pollution within the DOE. This amounted to an integrated approach to pollution control, an idea proposed as early as 1976 by the Royal Commission on Environmental Pollution. The Inspectorate was created following an efficiency study made by the Cabinet Office; its creation amounted to a "rationalization" of existing government machinery rather than the creation of a new administrative system; there was some question about whether the resources allocated to controlling pollution under HMIP were adequate to the task.[43] Certainly its subsequent record did not bode well. In the eighteen months to December 1989, three of its most senior officials resigned, and the Inspectorate was understaffed and demoralized.[44]

The second phase of environmental policy under Thatcher began (in the public arena at least) on 27 September 1988, with a speech by the Prime Minister to the Royal Society. In that speech, she outlined such problems as population growth, global warming, threats to the ozone layer and acid pollution, announced that her government espoused the concept of sustainable development, and argued that "stable prosperity can be achieved throughout the world provided the environment is nurtured and safeguarded. Protecting this balance of nature is therefore one of the great challenges of the late twentieth century."

On 14 October, during her keynote speech to the Conservative Party conference in Brighton, she argued that

> we Conservatives ... are not merely friends of the Earth – we are its guardians and trustees for generations to come. The core of Tory philosophy and the case for protecting the environment are the same. No generation has a freehold on this Earth. All we have is a life tenancy – with a full repairing lease. And this Government intends to meet the terms of that lease in full.[45]

Mrs Thatcher reinforced her statements by calling an international ozone layer conference in London in February 1989; the expenses of all the government delegations attending were paid by the British government. She also helped ensure that the environment was given prominent attention – for the first time – at the July 1989 economic summit in Paris. However, both in her October conference speech and at the Paris summit, she was careful to tie her warnings on the dangers of global warming to a promotion of nuclear power as an alternative source of energy.

In July 1989, Mrs Thatcher replaced Nicholas Ridley at the DOE with Chris Patten, who – in marked contrast to Ridley – was generally accepted by the environmental lobby as having relatively strong sympathies with the objectives of the lobby. Upon his appointment, Patten made much of his past links with interest groups. He also appointed as a part-time adviser Dr David Pearce, director of the London Environmental Economics Centre. A report written by Pearce on the economic underpinnings of sustainable development was published, arguing that it was a feasible, practical concept, and that it could be productively combined with economic policy.[46]

Patten also considered proposals for the creation of an independent Environment Protection Commission, responsible for controlling all forms of pollution, enforcing environmental protection and protecting wildlife and the countryside. An earlier recommendation for just such a commission had been rejected by Nicholas Ridley. In addition, proposals for a new Environment Protection Bill were outlined in the 1989 Queen's Speech, and a white paper was planned for late 1990. Mrs Thatcher herself chaired the cabinet committee overseeing the writing of the white paper, and a small group of senior civil servants was assembled within the DOE as a white paper directorate.

There is little question that Mrs Thatcher's two speeches had considerable public and political impact. Martin Jacques argues that with the Royal Society speech, concern for the environment was no longer the preserve of the environmental movement. With the speech, the environment made the transition

> from political marginality to political mainstream. . . . The environmental movement has been an outsider, an intruder. If little else happens, her speech will have the immediate effect of legitimizing the latter, and of making concern about the environment official.[47]

Tom Burke agrees:

> The Thatcher speeches were a milestone. They legitimized the environmental issue, and the game has now changed. Many more people will listen to Mrs Thatcher than to environmental groups. The groups created a receptive atmosphere by raising public consciousness, but now politicians are doing that. What is left for the groups to do?[48]

Mrs Thatcher's autumn 1988 speeches and her subsequent actions on the environment looked to many like some kind of conversion on the road to Damascus. From a position of hostility (or at least indifference) towards environmental management, she was now apparently a champion of environmentalism. This immediately raised two questions in the minds of her critics in the environmental movement: *had* she in fact undergone a conversion, and if so, *why* had she undergone a conversion? There is still no certain answer to the first question. Nicholas Ridley, for one, felt that there had been no change of policy; following the autumn 1988 speeches, he said: "There is no question of any kind of conversion." The environment had barely been mentioned in the Conservative election manifesto in 1987. As often as not, Mrs Thatcher continued during her last administration to respond rather than to take the initiative on environmental issues: water pollution controls were only improved because of a combination of EC law and the public debate surrounding water privatization; she was only forced to shelve her pro-nuclear policy once the costs of nuclear power became irrefutable; and she only agreed to action on acid pollution because of requirements under European Community law.

She also continued to promote the reduction of central government involvement in public services, and the reduction of manpower and funds for long-term research. Nicholas Ridley remained in place for nearly a year as environment secretary after Mrs Thatcher's autumn 1988 speeches, and there were indications that he was pursuing a programme aimed at weakening the state conservation agencies and the influence of the environmental lobby. A proposal made in July 1989 by Ridley that the NCC and the Countryside Commission be broken up, and its Scottish and Welsh responsibilities be given to new, separate bodies, met with considerable criticism from environmental groups and opposition parties. There were concerns that this would dissipate financial resources and scientific expertise, and promote local environmental interests at the expense of national interests. The proposal was tabled by Nicholas Ridley without any consultation with the chairman of the NCC, Sir William Wilkinson. There was some suspicion at the time that the proposal may have been aimed at weakening the power of an increasingly effective NCC, or that it was an attempt to help win back the Conservative vote in Scotland and Wales.[49]

By early 1990, there were further suspicions that Mrs Thatcher's "greenness" was beginning to be diluted. The *Economist* noted that early drafts of the white paper on the environment suggested that the administration's definition of environmental policy was unclear, that the Pearce Report's recommendations on using economic mechanisms to drive green policies were being overlooked and that the Prime Minister had lost her earlier enthusiasm for environmental policies. Stronger policies would increase public spending, something to which she had always been opposed, and she was now even more opposed given rising inflation and a worsening trade deficit.[50]

For those who believed that her mind *had* been changed, it became something of a game to try to identify the chief influence. Among those credited: President Reagan, because of his close relationship with Mrs Thatcher and his concerns about the 1988 Midwestern drought and possible links with global warming; the American scientist James Hansen, a member of the Goddard Institute for Space Studies, and one of a group of scientists who made a presentation to Mrs Thatcher in 1988; the British nuclear industry, which provided new data on global warming; and the Policy Unit at 10 Downing Street. Some believe that she may have been influenced because of her training in the natural sciences;[51] others believe that this was not the case.[52]

The individual most often mentioned in these musings was Sir Crispin Tickell, then British representative at the United Nations. A historian by training but an amateur naturalist by inclination, Tickell was a confidant of Mrs Thatcher, and may have had some influence on her. It is also possible that she may simply have been responding to the demands of the European Commission and other international agencies. Other less plausible explanations give credit to the growing attention in the media to environmental issues, and the growing attention paid to such issues by the opposition parties.

For Martin Jacques, the cause of the shift in Conservative thinking lay primarily with heightened public attention to environmental issues during 1988, caused by mounting concern over the greenhouse effect and threats to the ozone layer, the tragedy of the death of seals in the North Sea and controversy over the *Karin B*, a ship carrying a cargo of toxic waste which tried to offload the waste in Britain. The process, he argued, was helped by a growing body of informed opinion which took the matter seriously, not least in the scientific community.[53]

Jonathon Porritt, director of Friends of the Earth at the time and someone also (wrongly) credited with having changed Mrs Thatcher's mind, believes that the Department of the Environment had very little influence on Mrs Thatcher, beyond the attempts made by former environment minister William Waldegrave and his chief scientist, Martin Holdgate, to draw attention to issues such as acid pollution. Both had worked hard to promote environmental issues in the government in the mid-1980s; their departure in 1988 (Waldegrave to the Foreign Office, Holdgate to Switzerland to become director-general of the International Union for Conservation of Nature) was met with dismay on the part of environmental groups.

Tom Burke of the Green Alliance is adamant that environmental groups played no part at all in changing Mrs Thatcher's mind. He was one of a small group of environmentalists invited to a Downing Street meeting with Mrs Thatcher in 1985. "She quickly decided we were a bunch of amateurs who didn't know what we wanted," he recalls.[54] Andy Wilson of CPRE disagrees, arguing that groups made the environment into a vote-winning issue, and so had an indirect influence on Mrs Thatcher.[55] David Baldock agrees: "Environmental groups had a strong effect, partly because there was so much media coverage of environmental issues, and most of that had emanated from the groups. They set the debate."[56] Jonathon Porritt is quite certain about the role of environmental groups:

> The role of groups was fundamental. Before the politicization of the environment in 1988, environmental groups *were* the opposition to Thatcher in this country. They worked with ministers, they lobbied backbenchers, they worked with the media, they raised consciousness among the public. Parties weren't to be seen anywhere. The opposition was made up of environmental groups, which is one of the reasons why Mrs Thatcher has such a deep dislike of them. They had a considerable influence.[57]

Mrs Thatcher's interest in the environment was also almost certainly influenced by her views on Britain's place in the world. A renewed "national purpose" for Britain had always been a central part of Thatcherism (hence Marquand's description of Thatcherism as "a sort of British Gaullism"). In a 1981 speech, she said: "I want this nation to continue to be heard in the world and for the leaders of other countries to know that our strength comes from shared convictions as to what is right and wrong."[58] Alan Murie believes that some of Thatcher's enthusiasm for environmental issues can be ascribed in part to making "a merit of responses required" under European Community legislation.[59] Many environmentalists believe that positive statements on the global environment helped strengthen her position as an international statesperson. David Baldock comments that Mrs Thatcher was concerned about being overtaken on the world environmental stage by other leaders, such as François Mitterrand, Ruud Lubbers, Helmut Kohl and George Bush, but mainly by Mikhail Gorbachev.[60] Tom Burke concurs, suggesting that the speeches were provoked by Mrs Thatcher's fears that Gorbachev was "running away with the hearts and minds of Europe, especially West Germany", and that there was an absence of leadership on the international environment. By making positive statements on the environment, Mrs Thatcher may have hoped to make Germany better disposed towards Britain and the Community.[61]

Generally, there is a belief that Mrs Thatcher significantly changed her environmental policies only at the international level.[62] Jonathon Porritt suggests that making statements on the international environment involved far fewer policy commitments than statements on the domestic environment. He agrees that her statements involved the issue of international kudos, and that Mrs Thatcher saw herself as the leading politician of the Western world, especially after the departure of Ronald Reagan:

> She likes to portray herself as the pre-eminent defender of Western democracies. In order to perform at that level, she has to have a persona which is more than just a defence of the UK economy against France and Italy. She couldn't go down the disarmament route, which had already been claimed by Gorbachev. So I suspect that in terms of developing the right international image, the environment was one of the best ways in which she could achieve credibility and kudos. The ozone conference was a safe, high-profile international event that portrayed her in the best possible light.[63]

In the months following her autumn 1988 speeches, few environmentalists felt they could see much evidence of Mrs Thatcher's statements being converted into genuine political change at the domestic level (other than through unanticipated circumstances beyond her control – see Chapter 5). David Baldock argues that the Thatcher administration made concessions only on issues that cost little or nothing, such as reductions in CFC production.[64] Nigel Haigh believes that Mrs Thatcher understood that the environment was a major issue, but that she had not worked out the implications of environmental policy for other issues she believed in, such as freedom of choice, non-intervention and free markets.[65]

In a detailed assessment published in February 1989, Friends of the Earth described environmental policy-making in Britain since 1979 as "impoverished".[66] In an assessment published to mark the first anniversary of the Royal Society speech, Media Natura noted that, while it would have been unreasonable to expect substantial results from new policies within a year,

> the picture is not encouraging . . . [A] series of strategic decisions have been taken which set the UK on the course of more, not less, environmental degradation. Where progress has been made it is almost invariably, and grudgingly, at the behest of the European Commission or other international agencies.[67]

Andy Wilson of CPRE, while noting that the third Thatcher administration was greener than previous British administrations, felt that much more was needed, and that the Thatcher record could still only be described as "abysmal".[68]

Tom Burke argues that the lack of changes in domestic policy suggested that there was little will to match rhetoric with action:

> No one doubts that Mrs Thatcher is serious about the issues, but she knows that there is a domestic political price to be paid for her postures on the international environment. She says she sees the greenhouse effect as a major threat; at the same time, her energy secretary Cecil Parkinson announces that he is going to leave it to market forces to deliver greater energy efficiency, and her transport secretary Paul Channon announces that traffic in Britain might grow by 142 per cent in the next 30 years and Britain will be spending billions of pounds to make sure that it can. Never mind the consequences for global warming.[69]

Conclusions

Mrs Thatcher came to office in 1979 without a policy on the environment, and during her first two administrations was generally seen by environmentalists as unsympathetic to their goals. Interest groups generally were dismissed as subversive by Mrs Thatcher, as a primary example of the dangers of consensus politics and as one of the causes of the British disease. As someone opposed to government involvement in industry, Mrs Thatcher was generally opposed to the kind of regulation demanded by the environmental lobby.

In the autumn of 1988, she made two speeches which seemed to indicate a radical reversal of her previous position. Whatever the motives and sincerity behind her apparent new-found interest in the environment, there can be little doubt that her statements helped give environmental policy a new public prominence. For many, her statements finally gave legitimacy to the environmental lobby, and contributed towards making the environment a prominent issue on the British public policy agenda. Her statements also strengthened the environmental lobby by setting down a precise benchmark from which her subsequent actions could be measured more precisely. In other words, she created a new issue for herself to which a response was required.

4. Environmental Groups and the Countryside

For Britain, the most controversial and widely debated environmental issue of the postwar years – and perhaps of the twentieth century – has been the threat posed to the countryside by modern farming. The controversy has particularly gathered momentum since the debate over the Wildlife and Countryside Bill, which became an Act of Parliament in 1981. The bill focused unprecedented attention on an incipient disagreement between the agricultural and environmental lobbies. It emphasized the influence enjoyed by the agricultural lobby in the hallways of the Ministry of Agriculture, Fisheries and Food (MAFF), and revealed the relative lack of influence of conservation groups (a subsection of the environmental lobby concerned mainly with wildlife and countryside issues). However, the debate over the bill may have been the swan-song of the farming lobby. In the years that followed, environmentalists won new influence and public sympathy at the expense of the farming lobby. British farmers still enjoy many privileges, and many exclusions from planning laws, but the farming lobby today is neither as powerful nor as credible as it was in 1980.

Principles of the agricultural debate

The countryside and the rural ethic hold a place in the British psyche that is comparable to the position of forests in Germany or wilderness in the United States. Natural history, bird-watching and walks in the countryside are popular pastimes; access to amenity and the countryside is a continuing demand of individuals and interest groups; nature is a consistent theme and source of inspiration for artists. Yet ironically, there is very little about the British landscape that is "natural". Social and economic change over six thousand years or more has produced a landscape characterized by small fields and meadows divided by hedgerows, copses and small areas of woodland but more recently often converted into large arable prairies. It has also removed all but 7 per cent of the natural forest cover of the British Isles, and driven many animal and plant species into extinction. Very little true wilderness remains, and visits to Sherwood Forest, the New Forest and the Forest of Dean reveal only the vestiges of once great natural forests. For the rest, wildlife in the densely populated islands of Britain must live alongside farming. Farmers manage 85 per cent of all the rural land in Britain. For most of them, the priority is to "improve" and develop the land and to increase their output and efficiency.

For their motives, one must look back to the Second World War, when an agricultural revolution was launched aimed at making Britain self-sufficient in food. Before the war, Britain had seen a century of steady agricultural decline, and steadily increasing reliance on imported food. By 1939, Britain was importing about 70 per cent of its food needs: wheat from Canada and the United States, beef from Argentina, sugar cane from the Caribbean, and so on. Then came the German U-boat blockade in the early years of the war, quickly emphasizing the dangers of reliance on imported food. Realizing the strategic importance of food, the government launched a programme of agricultural intensification which has been maintained ever since. Yet more intensification was encouraged after 1970 by guaranteed prices made available under the European Community's Common Agricultural Policy. These guarantees meant that farmers could sell whatever they produced, irrespective of levels of production and demand. With such incentives, farmers throughout Europe were encouraged to produce more than consumers needed, and the result was that the Community began to stockpile huge surpluses of butter, skimmed milk, cheese, beef, wine, wheat and barley.

By the late 1970s, British agriculture had become big business. Marion Shoard argues that agriculture had become as much of an industry as manufacturing, "involving cash-flow calculations, the use of machines rather than men – and massive subsidy from the taxpayer".[1] These subsidies encouraged farmers to use all the land they had, and to "reclaim" previously uncultivable land in order to produce more. In order to do this, they needed to create bigger fields. That meant cutting down hedgerows and forests and reclaiming wetlands at an unprecedented rate; between 1946 and 1974, a quarter of the hedgerows in England and Wales – about 120,000 miles in all – were removed. It also meant increased pollution from crop spraying and straw burning, and an increased risk of soil erosion over large areas of arable land.

For many conservationists, farming by the late 1970s no longer enriched the landscape, but destroyed it. Richard Munton observes that the controversy had reached the point by the early 1980s where there was no longer any serious debate about whether or not modern farming conflicted with amenity and wildlife; instead, the focus of the discussion had moved on to how the conflict could be resolved.[2] As farming became big business, the traditional view of the farmer as a sturdy yeoman who best understood the needs of the countryside was increasingly challenged by conservation groups, who concentrated many of their efforts on drawing public attention to the extent of changes in the countryside. There was much concern about the conversion of the British landscape to large, featureless prairies. Deciduous forests had been steadily replaced by commercial conifer plantations or converted to arable land; between 1947 and 1980, half the ancient woodlands in Britain were lost in this way. Grasslands, bogs, marshes, heaths, downs and moorlands have been similarly converted.

The nature of the changes in the countryside was described in 1974 by Richard Westmacott and Tom Worthington in *New Agricultural Landscapes*, a study which was neither scientific nor comprehensive, but which drew attention to the inadequacy of controls over land use.[3] Debate over the issue intensified during the 1970s as more studies were published reaching conclusions similar to those of Westmacott and Worthington. Among the most influential of these was *The Theft of the Countryside*, written by Marion Shoard and published in 1980. She noted that Britain's planning system was widely considered the most sophisticated and effective mechanism in the world for curbing the inherent tendency of powerful private interests to override public interest in land. Despite that, it was doing almost nothing to safeguard landscape from the systematic onslaught of modern agriculture.

> The planning system does not attempt to reconcile the different priorities of food production and landscape or wildlife conservation in cases where the two interests conflict. . . . [Farming and commercial forestry] are effectively above the law as it applies to other activities which affect the environment.[4]

The debate was taken further in 1982 with the publication of *Agriculture: The Triumph and the Shame* by Richard Body. Body criticized the system of agricultural support for doing damage in Britain (and elsewhere in the world) for "the sake of short-term and often illusory gains".[5] As well as adding to the argument against farmers, the book was particularly notable for the fact that it was written by a Conservative MP representing a rural constituency, and himself a farmer and member of the National Farmers' Union. Richard Howarth describes the book as "the spark [that kindled] the fire of a far-reaching public debate".[6] As a result of the book, the Centre for Agricultural Strategy and the Centre for European Agricultural Studies convened a conference on countryside issues in 1983.

For two conservationists – Charlie Pye-Smith and Chris Rose – the new debate over the countryside emphasized a fundamental weakness in the conservation movement. Writing in 1984, they argued that the effective conservation of the countryside demanded "drastic changes" in the workings of the farming, forestry and water businesses.

> What is so sad is that many conservationists . . . have persistently

> clung to the belief that farming and conservation share the same interests, aims and objectives. . . . While the conservationists have pursued this softly-softly approach of 'consensus, cooperation and compromise'. . . the landowning interests have done just the opposite.[7]

In fact, faith in this consensus approach may have already begun to dim by the early 1980s. The sympathetic and positive image of farming promoted by *The Archers* no longer seemed particularly real to conservationists. Not only were many farmers now being seen as unsympathetic to conservation, but serious questions were being raised about the nature of agricultural policy and the influence of the farming lobby in the deliberations of MAFF.

The Thatcherite enterprise culture, with its emphasis on eliminating waste and encouraging business to stand on its own two feet, might have prompted more discussion about agricultural policy in the early 1980s, but Mrs Thatcher was too concerned during her first administration with inflation to pay much attention to agricultural issues.[8] Thatcherism also encompassed a desire to cut public expenditure, however, and Mrs Thatcher *did* pay close attention to renegotiating the British contribution to the European Community. Britain paid in a great deal more than it received, largely because of the Common Agricultural Policy (CAP). Among other things, the CAP placed levies on food imported from outside the EC (Britain had relatively extensive trade with non-EC countries, such as New Zealand), and spent huge sums on guaranteed prices to farmers. Relatively few of the payments made under the CAP were received by British farmers, because there are fewer British farmers in comparison to consumers than is the case in Germany or France.

Mrs Thatcher's concerns regarding the CAP were purely financial, and came as a result of her programme of reducing public spending. She was not particularly motivated by a desire to reform agricultural policy. The notion of subsidies and state price supports may run counter to the very notion of free-enterprise Thatcherism, yet the Thatcher administration played a notably marginal role in the agricultural debate, not least because of fears of alienating voters in the Tory shires. In fact, it lacked a countryside policy altogether. Conservationists feared that, if anything, the administration wanted to reduce planning controls on farming, and open up new economic opportunities in the countryside.

During 1986, for example, a number of government departments (including MAFF, the DOE, the Treasury and the departments of employment and trade and industry) were involved in the preparation of a study called *Alternative Land Uses and the Rural Economy* (*ALURE*). All those food surpluses had led to much farmland being surplus to needs, raising the idea that the government might think about alternative uses for this land. Leaks to the press about the content of the study raised fears among conservationists that the government was planning to encourage new leisure developments in the countryside, which would pose yet more threats to nature. The National Farmers' Union meanwhile pressed for additional subsidies to keep land out of production. The study led in early 1987 to something of a power struggle between the Ministry of Agriculture and the DOE over which had ultimate responsibility over countryside policy, and to concerns among Conservatives that the Thatcher administration would end up alienating many farmers.

Examples such as this excepted, the countryside debate has been less an ideological issue – involving a response on the part of interest groups to Conservative Party policy – than a struggle involving a concerned conservation lobby addressing itself to a bureaucratic system based on a privileged relationship between the regulators (MAFF) and the regulated (the National Farmers' Union). Caught in the midst of this relationship have been two relatively powerless state conservation agencies: the Countryside Commission (CC) and the Nature Conservancy Council (NCC). The nature of this power struggle says much about the role and relative powers of competing interest groups in designing and/or influencing policy in Britain. At the heart of the debate are two of the most fundamental and recurring dilemmas faced by environmental policy-makers: first, the struggle between those who want to exploit natural resources for short-term economic gain, and those who want to use the resources sustainably for long-term, continuing productivity; and secondly, the prominence given economic interests over environmental interests in the consultation process.

The rise of the conservation debate

In order to understand conservation policy in Britain, it helps first to contrast British attitudes to pollution control and countryside planning. There are three fundamental differences.

- First, where pollution control has traditionally been shrouded in secrecy, and has involved voluntary compliance and agreements between the regulators and the regulated, decisions on land use are highly visible, providing many opportunities for public participation. One result is that environmental groups have been much more active over the years in challenging policy decisions on countryside issues than on pollution issues.
- Secondly, and partly as a function of their relative openness, land planning policies have often been contentious and controversial.
- Finally, because changes in the countryside have often been more visible than pollution, and because people have understood less about the causes and consequences of pollution, the British public has traditionally been much more concerned about countryside issues than about pollution, although this has changed in recent years (see Chapter 5).

Britain has one of the most comprehensive planning systems in the world. Dating from 1890, when local authorities were given powers to remove slums and build new housing, a growing body of legislation has extended the powers of central and local government over land use. The existing system is largely the result of a series of town and country planning Acts passed since the 1920s; the most important of these was the 1947 Town and Country Planning Act.

All land in England is owned by the Crown; there is no absolute private ownership of the land. Individuals have certain rights over that land, but others are also given the right of access (for example, to fish, quarry minerals or cross the land along public footpaths). The 1947 Act introduced a new principle: that new development and changes in the use of land were to be subject to control aimed at ensuring conformity to development plans prepared by local planning authorities. Since 1947, the right to develop land has been vested in the state. Anyone wanting to "develop" their land must apply to the local planning authority for permission. If the authority refuses, the applicant has the right to appeal to the Department of the Environment (since 1970), which can overrule the local authority.

In theory, this system is designed to let people do whatever they want with the land over which they have freehold, so long as their plans do not materially harm the community. In practice, Marion Shoard argues,

> the system gives the interests of people other than the freeholder far less of a hearing in the countryside. A farmer may convert rough moor, heath or down to wheat prairie, clear away hedgerows and trees, put streams underground, and drain and enclose marshes without even notifying, let alone seeking the views of, the rest of the community.[9]

Shoard notes that farming was exempted from planning controls in 1947 "because it hardly occurred to anybody to include it . . . planners and conservationists saw agriculture as something that needed to be protected rather than as a potentially destructive force".[10] Some conservationists even went so far as to see agricultural Britain as part of the beauty of the countryside. The CPRE, for example, saw farming as an activity which *conserved* the countryside; for them, the main threats to nature came from urban development and mining operations. Since the Second World War, however, conservationists have increasingly come to look on farming as a threat to wildlife and the countryside.

All these concerns came to a head during the planning and

passage of the 1981 Wildlife and Countryside Act. The Act was passed to meet British obligations resulting from the 1979 EC Directive on the conservation of wild birds. The Directive had in turn been agreed as a result of growing public concern about the annual slaughter of migratory birds in southern Europe, and was itself drawn up in consultation with the Royal Society for the Protection of Birds (RSPB). From the mid-1970s, the RSPB had become ever more closely concerned with European wildlife issues, in addition to its domestic concerns. The Society's European officer was appointed to the European Commission's expert committee overseeing implementation of the Directive, and adoption of the Directive involved the RSPB in lengthy consultations with the DOE, helping establish good working relations between the two.[11]

The consultative stages of the Act involved much discussion between the DOE, MAFF, the Country Landowners' Association (CLA) and the National Farmers' Union (NFU). There was little involvement of either the Countryside Commission or the NCC, however, and – with the exception of RSPB input – almost no consultation with the environmental lobby. So while the interests of the CLA and NFU were well represented and largely met, those of the conservation lobby were not. Unusually, the Wildlife and Countryside Bill was introduced first in the House of Lords. The conservation lobby – which was poorly prepared and organized at the outset of the debate – took the opportunity to work through its contacts in the Lords for substantial amendments to the bill. Their response was co-ordinated by a new Wildlife Link Committee convened by Lord Melchett, the Labour peer (subsequently to become director of Greenpeace).

The bill made provision for compensatory payments to farmers if their land was managed less economically for environmental reasons. It was based on the voluntary compliance of those being regulated – in this case, the farmers. Local authorities were to make the payments, supported by grants from the Countryside Commission. While some saw the bill as a step forward in the protection of specialist wildlife habitats, the Act as passed suffered many anomalies and inherent weaknesses. First, neither local nor central government has been able to commit sufficient resources to the programme of payments. Secondly, the Act did not prevent existing or future owners of Sites of Special Scientific Interest from earning compensatory payments simply by *threatening* to develop the sites. Within months of the passage of the Act, it became clear that it was insufficient, and there was strong support among environmental groups for its replacement.

The negotiations and consultation that took place during the consideration of the Wildlife and Countryside Bill saw frenetic activity on the part of interest groups. In all, it took several hundred hours of debate carried out over eleven months and resulting in a record 2,300 amendments before the Act was passed. The process also resulted in a fundamental long-term change in the outlook and tactics of the conservation lobby. Many MPs were made aware for the first time of the size and influence of the conservation movement. Bill Adams believes that the debate also had a sobering effect on environmental groups: "There was substantial NGO input into the debate over the Act, and that really taught the voluntary sector all about politics. It gave the conservation lobby a coherence that they haven't had since 1984."[12] Some argue that where conservation groups had previously seen themselves as being above party politics, their experiences during the debate on the Wildlife and Countryside Act drew them into the party arena; even the more conservative groups were provoked into a more demonstrative and adversarial position.[13] The debate also ended the consensus that had existed between the state agencies (the CC and NCC) and conservation groups. The groups felt renewed concern about what they saw as too much acquiescence on the part of the state agencies to government policy.

The decline of the farming lobby

At the time of the debate over the Wildlife and Countryside Act, the farming lobby enjoyed a level of influence over agricultural policy which stood in stark contrast to that of the conservation lobby. It is still in something of a privileged position today, since farmers are still exempted from many of the planning controls imposed on other sectors of the economy. However, since the passage of the Act, the overall influence and power of the farming lobby have declined as the influence of the conservation lobby has grown.

Many analyses of contemporary British politics refer to "policy communities" in which interest groups enjoy a partnership with government departments and statutory bodies in forming and implementing policy. Agricultural policy was determined in the early 1980s by just such a community. It was a community that was described in 1986 as "a remarkably closed one. It is a community in which a small number of interest groups . . . are highly significant, in some instances enjoying exclusive representation enshrined in statute."[14] Pre-eminent among these groups were the NFU and the CLA. Anyone looking closely at the operations of MAFF could see a clear bias towards consultation and negotiation with the NFU, rather than with conservation groups. Philip Lowe argues that the power and influence of the NFU did not come from the inherent economic power of farmers, but rather from the strong relationship allowed by the government.[15] This influence dated from the 1947 Act, which required the government, when setting agricultural price support levels, to consult "such bodies of persons who appear to them to represent the interests of producers in the agricultural industry". Agriculture has been described as the one unequivocal example of an economic sector where an interest group has been officially recognized by the state and incorporated into the process of decision-making.[16]

By the late 1970s, the relationship between the NFU and MAFF was so strong that contacts between the two were taking place on a daily, sometimes even an hourly, basis. The NFU has been described as "the textbook example of the influential group".[17] Writing in 1977, Gerald Wilson noted that while consultation with affected interests may have been normal in the British system, the relationship between MAFF and the NFU was "far closer than is normal".[18] The leaders of the NFU, he argued,

> used their autonomy to maintain close and friendly relations with government in general and MAFF in particular. They have behaved less politically, more moderately, and more like an extension of the Civil Service than many of their members would have wished.[19]

Des Wilson was less guarded in his opinions of the NFU, suggesting that the Union had succeeded in perpetuating "the most outrageously generous deal towards farmers and the most appalling economic and agricultural policies with virtually no opposition"; he believed it was one of the key roles of conservation groups to oppose interest groups such as the NFU.[20]

Founded in 1908, the NFU grew rapidly after the Second World War, becoming by the mid-1970s one of Britain's most powerful and efficient interest groups. More than 80 per cent of British farmers were members, and the Union had much greater resources and better access to policy-makers than the conservation groups which were its rivals. Not only did it have a well-run and comprehensive media programme, and close contacts with MAFF, but it also had much influence over rural district councils, many of whose members were farmers. It also had regular contact with about a hundred MPs, helped by the fact that many MPs and cabinet ministers were also farmers or landowners.[21]

Marion Shoard argues that the NFU took the attitude that farmers knew what was best for the countryside, and that those who disputed the right of farmers lacked an understanding of the intricacies of farming, and were therefore ignorant and naïve.[22] She also notes that the NFU was able to remain independent of the main political parties because of the absence of party political differences on the conflict between agriculture and conservation.[23] British governments since the war had been committed to intervention in farming, so long as it did not require the nationalization of land, but left farming in the hands of a set of small private operators.

Finer argues that "a close relationship tends to become a closed one".[24] While some suggest that the image of the NFU as an insider organization may have been exaggerated,[25] others have fewer doubts. Des Wilson, for example, described the relationship in 1985 as follows:

> You've got a Ministry that has been working with the NFU for so long that they talk the same language; they go to the same clubs and eat in the same restaurants. They know each other on first name terms. ... Friends of the Earth has done all the research on pesticides ... [yet] the Government is talking to farmers and the chemical industry in formulating legislative plans. They're not talking to us, we are not on the inside there, we are not part of the club.[26]

Providing a stark contrast to its close relationship with the farming community, MAFF generally proved unresponsive to the demands of the conservation community in the 1970s and early 1980s. The only exception was its relations with the Farming and Wildlife Advisory Group (FWAG). FWAG was set up in 1969 by MAFF, the NFU, the RSNC and the RSPB to promote the reconciliation of farming and conservation through regular one-day conferences and other events. While this may have seemed like a public-spirited move on the part of MAFF, support for FWAG undeniably had a number of advantages for MAFF:[27]

- It could counter any criticism from conservationists by pointing to its support for FWAG as evidence of its commitment to conservation.
- Through FWAG, conservation opinion was made readily accessible to MAFF.
- FWAG's policy position was that farming and conservation were not incompatible, and could be reconciled by providing suitable advice, information and incentives for farmers to include conservation in their planning and management. By supporting this policy, MAFF could avoid questions of agricultural policy reform.
- FWAG defined a moderate middle ground, giving more influence to the establishment-oriented and more conservative interest groups that were members, while marginalizing the more radical groups which were not members (such as

Friends of the Earth), or those which had pressed for agricultural policy reform (such as the Ramblers' Association and CPRE).

Conservation groups neither had the same level of access to MAFF as the NFU or the CLA, nor possessed the power of veto that would automatically ensure them a place in the agricultural policy community. However, they did have a number of tactics which had been used to effect to achieve particular objectives.[28] First, groups could use public censure by generating a body of public opinion, using the conservation lobby's good contacts with the media. These contacts were occasionally so effective as to prompt complaints from the CLA that tales of environmental destruction captured headlines much more effectively than the reporting of "good conservation news".[29] Secondly, groups could attempt to block or delay the implementation of policy, particularly during the public consultation stage of the planning process. Public inquiries had provided interest groups with many opportunities to challenge policy and delay implementation.

Thirdly, outsider groups could form coalitions with insider groups for tactical purposes, as Transport 2000 did in the 1970s by forming a partnership with railway unions. FWAG provides an example of a similar strategy, although its effectiveness was severely limited. Farmers and the NFU proved a notably united group, allowing little opportunity for conservation groups to woo sub-factions, such as small farmers or hill farmers. Increased specialization in the wake of EC membership, however, tended to cause a rift between arable farmers and livestock producers,[30] suggesting the increased possibility of tactical coalitions in the future. Finally, with the back-door method, groups could try to enlist the support of a "friendly" department in their negotiations with an "unfriendly" department. Thus groups tried to win the support of the DOE and the statutory agencies in discussions with MAFF.

Following the passage of the Wildlife and Countryside Act, there was – not surprisingly – a strong desire on the part of conservation groups to end the monopoly over agricultural policy-making enjoyed by the NFU–CLA–MAFF triumvirate. To a large extent, this monopoly *has* been weakened since 1981. Groups have been helped by a new climate of public opinion that is more sceptical about the claims of the farming lobby than before, and more supportive of a comprehensive, rational countryside policy. This sea-change has in turn been encouraged by several different factors.

First, there has been political and public concern over the financial costs of agricultural policy and over surplus production. Although many people may not have understood the intricacies of the rebates from the EC sought by Mrs Thatcher in the early 1980s, few were opposed to the idea of Britain paying less to support a policy that seemed hugely inefficient and wasteful. The British – many of whom are still reluctant Europeans at best – would also have been more than willing to point to the obscenity of agricultural surpluses in Europe at a time when much of the less developed world was either short of food or starving.

Secondly, the conservation lobby has been successful in drawing public attention to changes in the countryside. Especially in the wake of the Wildlife and Countryside Act, public concern about the countryside grew. This was reflected, for example, in the remarkable growth in membership and funding enjoyed by the biggest conservation groups during the 1980s (see Chapter 8).

Thirdly, there has been a marked demographic change in Britain involving a growing population shift in the second half of the 1980s away from the cities and towards rural areas. There are numerous causes behind this change. There has been a decline of manufacturing industries tied to sources of raw materials such as coal and iron, and hence a shift away from the old industrial centres of the Midlands and the North. There has been a marked growth in financial services that need not be based in cities. Commuter catchment areas have been extended, with people driving or taking public transport over greater distances to go to and from work; many commuters have moved from city suburbs to towns, villages or the country itself. Allied to this, there has been a growth in country-based jobs, and the advent of the "electronic cottage" has allowed more people to spend more time working from their homes.

All these changes have combined to cause a decline in urban populations, and a growth in the population of rural counties. Between 1981 and 1988, for example, the population of counties in a band from Cornwall to Norfolk grew by 6 per cent or more. These changes have in turn had a number of effects: more people now have a direct, vested interest in the welfare of the countryside; more people are directly experiencing the changes about which the conservation lobby has been warning; the rural vote is more important; and farmers account for proportionately fewer of the total rural population.

Fourthly, there has been growing volume of criticism directed at MAFF by sectors of media and government. For example, the 1984 House of Lords select committee on the European Communities condemned MAFF for being too "backward-looking", too oriented towards production and insufficiently responsive to public opinion on the countryside.[31] The 1984 Lords committee on science and technology expressed concern at the lack of research on the long-term environmental implications of modern farming and forestry, caused by research priorities being dominated by the interests of the farming and food industries.[32] The 1985 Commons select committee on the environment accused MAFF officials of being "half-hearted" over conservation, and of not responding to public opinion on the issue of the imbalance between agriculture and the environment.[33]

Finally, a number of public controversies over the morality of modern farming practices and the quality of agricultural produce served in the late 1980s to reduce the credibility of farmers and modern agriculture. The debate over factory farming has led many to question the moral values of modern agriculture, and to make new demands for organic produce and free-range eggs. This was helped in the late 1980s by several well-publicized and expensive incidents involving food and health. Concerns over salmonella briefly became a national *cause célèbre* in late 1988 with the assertion by Edwina Currie, the junior health minister, that most British egg production was "affected with salmonella". The issue resulted in the resignation of Mrs Currie in December, but attention had already been drawn to fears about shortcomings in food quality standards and the increasing incidence of cases of food poisoning in all industrialized countries.

Additional controversies over botulism and listeria were followed in early 1990 by a public scare over bovine spongiform encephalopathy (BSE, or "mad cow disease"). The BSE controversy had two particular effects: first, it accelerated the decline in public confidence in farmers and farming; secondly, it subjected MAFF to much criticism for its poor handling of the issue. The *Economist*, for example, noted that the controversy had "proved beyond scientific doubt that nobody trusts MAFF any more", and that BSE "belongs to a sequence of food scandals that the ministry seems powerless to prevent. MAFF's performance is all the more lamentable because it had ample time to prepare its arguments."[34]

All these factors have combined to reduce public faith in farmers and farming. While public awareness about the changes taking place in the countryside continued to grow during the late 1980s, those changes have not gone away, and the government has continued to lack a clearly defined countryside policy. At the same time, there has also been a rather ironic reduction in public interest in the fate of the countryside. Since the 1970s (and earlier), some environmentalists had been arguing that the plight of wildlife and the countryside was a *symptom* of broader, underlying social and economic values, and that those values had to be changed if the countryside was to be protected. They began arguing that preventing the underlying causes of change in the countryside was better than trying to cure the effects. This view gained wider currency in the 1980s; as a result, there was a shift towards more concern for broader "quality of life" issues. More people began to question the values of a society that allowed environmental problems to emerge, and began examining their own values and lifestyles rather than simply blaming broader economic trends.

To some extent, this change may have been helped by the successes of the conservation lobby. Bill Adams argues that while conservation groups were undoubtedly bigger and wealthier at the end of the decade than they were at the beginning, they lacked coherence and direction; to some extent, the issue of the countryside had been institutionalized to the point where the countryside had become a career option rather than a political issue for many people.[35] This, he argues, was partly due to the fact that there were no major conservation controversies at the end of the 1980s that could have provided focus; the only minor exception was the public debate in 1989 over government plans to restructure the state conservation agencies.

The shift away from a focus on countryside issues may also have been due to a new level of public and political interest from late 1988 and early 1989 in global problems such as the greenhouse effect and threats to the ozone layer (see Chapter 5), and in consumer issues (see Chapter 6). Countryside issues tended to remain prominent only in so far as they related to questions of public health and ethics (such as the quality of food, and the debate over factory farming versus organic farming).

Conclusions

Changes made to the countryside by modern agricultural practices, and the threats thereby posed to species and habitat, have been the source of some of the most controversial environmental conflicts of the postwar years. Particularly since the late 1970s, there has been growing public and media attention paid to these issues. The political and economic forces that underlie agricultural change and land conversion have revealed much not only about the nature of the planning system in Britain, but also about the priorities of successive British governments. They have also drawn attention to a long-established, privileged relationship enjoyed by the farming lobby with the government.

Unlike pollution policy, which has been surrounded in secrecy, agricultural policy and land use issues are relatively open, and thus more subject to public debate. The efforts of environmental groups over the past fifteen to twenty years have been substantially aimed at drawing attention to the nature of the changes caused by agricultural intensification, and to what this says about the nature of the public policy process. Environmental groups have been particularly active in lobbying for the amendment of planned countryside legislation, their activities coming to a head at the time of the parliamentary debate over the 1981 Wildlife and Countryside Act. Having learned much about the political system and the means available to them to exert political influence, groups have continued to monitor government policy. They have been helped in their objectives by the gradual decline that has occurred during the 1980s in the power and influence of the farming lobby.

5. Privatization and Pollution

Protection of wildlife and the countryside has long been a popular issue in Britain, and the subject of active lobbying by interest groups. By contrast, pollution has attracted much less public attention. There are two reasons for this. First, the most visible form of air pollution – smoke – was addressed by the 1956 Clean Air Act. Other forms of air pollution have remained, and in some cases grown worse, but few are as visible as smoke. Secondly, and more importantly, the limited public interest in pollution issues, and the low level of opposition or public mobilization on the part of environmental groups, is due to the fact that Britain's pollution control has traditionally been based on a policy of non-coercive, voluntary compliance, and a "partnership" between the regulators (central and local government) and the regulated. Unlike planning decisions, which can be very public and visible, pollution control policy has been shrouded in secrecy.

Against this background, it was all the more surprising that air and water pollution should have become such prominent political and public issues in 1988–9. Not only did pollution attract extensive new media coverage, but more environmental groups began lobbying in the late 1980s in favour of tighter pollution control, and senior members of the Thatcher administration (including Margaret Thatcher herself) began taking an interest in pollution issues. Given her lack of any previous interest in pollution, the sight of Mrs Thatcher making public statements on global warming and convening a conference in

London on the ozone layer was remarkable.

Air pollution: emergence of an issue

As the first industrialized nation, Britain was also the first heavily polluted nation. John Evelyn was complaining as early as the seventeenth century about the "Hellish and dismall Cloud" which made London resemble "the suburbs of Hell".[1] Localized attempts were made to control some kinds of pollution in the early nineteenth century, but modern air pollution control in Britain really dates from the Alkali Act of 1863 and the creation of the Alkali Inspectorate. Controlling pollution from the alkali industry initially depended on the efforts of the Inspectorate, but it was helped by lobbying from interest groups, notably local groups in northern industrial cities, and by the National Smoke Abatement Institution, founded in 1880. In 1909, the northern groups came together to form the Smoke Abatement League. In 1929, the League coalesced with the Coal Smoke Abatement Society (founded in 1898) to form the National Smoke Abatement Society, renamed the National Society for Clean Air (NSCA) in 1958. (The final name change came in 1989, when the words "and Environmental Protection" were added to the title.) Some measure of the relative importance of countryside issues and pollution issues is the fact that the NSCA is the only national interest group working wholly on broad pollution issues, compared to at least thirty national organizations working wholly or substantially on wildlife and countryside issues.

The level of public understanding of air pollution issues in the nineteenth century was improved by the publication in 1880 of *London Fogs* by Rollo Russell, son of Lord John Russell[2]. This was the first time that widespread public attention had been drawn to the human cost of London fogs (actually, smogs – from an amalgam of smoke and fog). Public understanding and awareness were also promoted by visible and harmful pollution incidents. London smogs in particular caused growing concern. One in 1873 caused at least 270 (and possibly as many as 700) deaths, and another in 1880 caused between 700 and 1,100 deaths.[3] Yet despite the early successes of interest groups and the campaigning of interested members of Parliament, despite periodic attempts to strengthen pollution control laws and despite the obvious costs to health of air pollution, public opinion on air pollution remained relatively staid and uninformed until after the Second World War. By then, controls on noxious gases had been improved, but not those on smoke, grit and dust.[4] These remained the chief causes of air pollution, but had not been sufficiently controlled, for a number of reasons:

- Gases could be monitored quantitatively, while smoke could not.
- Gases were monitored by a team of experts, while smoke was left to overworked and poorly informed local public health officials.
- Gases were produced by relatively few identifiable sources, while smoke was produced by millions of private homes.
- Millions of private citizens were willing to tolerate smoke in order to have open coal fires.

It may have been a single event which ultimately did most to change public and political opinion. London had long been infamous for its "pea-souper" smogs, but from 5 to 13 December 1952 a particularly virulent smog settled on the city, causing an estimated 4,000 deaths (mainly among people already prone to air pollution, such as the very young, the elderly and people with a history of breathing problems). Estimates of the number of deaths were published in the *British Medical Journal* in January 1953, and the National Smoke Abatement Society (NSAS) conducted its own survey of the extent of damage, circulating the findings to MPs. Yet it was only in the spring of 1953 that the government finally acknowledged that an issue existed.[5] What made the 1952 smog different from earlier smogs was the extent of media interest; Derek Elsom argues that the smog "provided the trigger for the public and media to press the government into some form of action concerning the control of air pollution".[6]

Public concern was such that a committee of inquiry was set up under the chairmanship of Sir Hugh Beaver. Suspecting that this had been done largely to assuage public and media opinion, and concerned that the issue should not die, Beaver issued an interim report close to the first anniversary of the smog. This charged central government and local authorities with negligence in failing to take all possible steps to protect Londoners from the effects of smog, and also lay partial blame at the doorstep of consumers who continued to burn coal.[7] The recommendations of the Beaver Committee's final report in November 1954 were immediately accepted in principle by the government. Supported by briefings from the NSAS, a parliamentary campaign for a Clean Air Act was promoted by Sir Gerald Nabarro, leading to the passage of the Act in 1956.

Partly as a result of the Clean Air Act, smoke pollution over Britain fell visibly and rapidly; between 1960 and 1984 alone, annual emissions fell from 1.75 million tonnes to 300,000 tonnes.[8] The goals of the Act were helped by changes from gas to electricity, shifts in the population from cities to suburbs and the efforts of alkali inspectors.[9] However, while smoke emissions fell (the anti-smoke campaign having been helped by the fact that smoke is visible), emissions of invisible or less easily detectable pollutants such as sulphur dioxide (SO_2), nitrogen oxides (NOx), lead, carbon monoxide and hydrocarbons were less easily controlled. It was only in 1988 that action on SO_2 and NOx was agreed, and only in 1989 that lead-free petrol was finally made widely available in Britain (see Chapter 7). Despite this, pollutants such as nitrogen oxides, carbon monoxide, carbon dioxide and hydrocarbons remain a problem.

Principles of British pollution control policy

Pollution control policy in Britain stands in notable contrast to that of most other industrialized nations. While the United States, Germany and other European countries rely on enforceable air quality and emission standards, Britain relies instead on flexibility and consensus. This may change as the harmonization of European Community pollution control gathers pace, but so far, British pollution control has been based on tailoring standards to meet the particular circumstances of specific polluters and the local environment. Under the 1973 Water Act, for example, all sources of effluents discharged into virtually all bodies of water had first to be granted a consent by a Regional Water Authority. Each consent was individually negotiated with each polluter, and was tailor-made to reflect the kinds of substances being discharged, the capacity of the water system to absorb them and the ultimate disposition of the water supply.[10] As Tim O'Riordan notes, normal practice in Britain has been to leave the question of the extent to which polluters should be forced to clean up "to the good public sense of polluters in private consultation with regulatory officials".[11]

British pollution control policy traditionally has been based on three principles. The first is that of using the "best practicable means" to prevent pollution. This was first introduced into British law in 1842, the idea being that the government should interfere as little as possible with industry, while at the same time trying to placate public opinion.[12] Subsequently, the Alkali Inspectorate (renamed the Industrial Air Pollution Inspectorate in 1982, and incorporated into the new integrated HM Inspectorate of Pollution in 1987) was regularly criticized for bringing very few successful prosecutions against polluting industries. For example, there were only three prosecutions between 1920 and 1967.[13] To complicate matters, the term "practicable" has never been adequately defined; it is worked out on the basis of local conditions and circumstances, the state of technological knowledge and the costs of pollution control.[14]

The infrequency of prosecutions against polluters reflects the second principle of British pollution control: voluntary compliance. The Alkali Inspectorate saw itself as being in a partnership with industry, preferring to educate and persuade industrialists to adopt appropriate pollution control measures, rather than forcing them using the threat of prosecution.[15] Industries that did not come under the provisions of national law came under local authority control, where they were similarly "persuaded" through the use of "good emission conduct" codes. One feature of these policies has been the high level of consultation between government and industry on the setting and enforcement of goals and standards. The poacher and the gamekeeper have worked together to the extent that, in the 1970s, the Confederation of British Industry actually nominated several members to the boards of Regional Water Authorities.

The principle of voluntary compliance in turn relates to the third principle of pollution control in Britain: secrecy. In order to make voluntary compliance and the partnership between poachers and gamekeepers work, pollution control agencies have traditionally kept their discussions with industry confidential. This has had the effect of undermining public confidence in the position of government on pollution, but it has also made sure that pollution issues have been restricted to private rather than public negotiation.

Writing in 1986, David Vogel noted that "there is in Britain today no significant domestic pressure to change the way British pollution-control policy is either made or enforced".[16] There were several possible reasons for this. First, not only was there little public pressure to change the system, but hardly anyone even knew how the system operated. Most people had never heard of the Alkali Inspectorate, for example. Secondly, any potential criticism of the system was diffused by the decentralization of pollution control responsibilities, which also focused conflict at the local level. Thirdly, public concerns about pollution were diluted by the unquestionable and very visible improvement in the quality of Britain's air since the late 1950s.

Finally, the environmental lobby has not chosen to make pollution an issue. Until 1987, and with a few notable exceptions, few British environmental groups paid much attention to pollution issues. Given the way that pollution control policy was made and enforced, and the issues that most excited people, public opinion was much more likely to be mobilized by countryside issues than by pollution issues. Most British environmental groups have focused primarily on wildlife and countryside issues. If the environmental lobby is seen as the primary "opposition" and source of motivation for changes in public policy, then the lack of significant attention to pollution issues by environmental groups has meant that there has been much less pressure on the government to change policy on pollution than on protection of the countryside. Even for groups such as Friends of the Earth and Greenpeace, pollution has been only one of several issues they have addressed.

There was some interest shown by both public and policymakers in the growing movement in other European countries to control acid pollution during the early 1980s. However, the attempts made by the environmental lobby to draw public attention to the issue – and to encourage the British government to legislate to control acid pollution – were both sporadic and piecemeal. Acid pollution remained only a marginal issue in British policy thinking, and, as a public issue, achieved nothing like the status it did in West Germany and the Scandinavian countries.

Similarly, while the accident at Chernobyl in April 1986 caused concern throughout Europe about the consequences of radioactive fallout, and caused something of a crisis in confidence in the nuclear industry, concern in Britain was transient. Chernobyl did not lead to any substantial increase in demands by the environmental lobby for an end to the nuclear power programme, nor for the strengthening of air pollution controls more generally. In fact, the anti-nuclear movement in Britain has been much less active than in Germany or the United States. Philip Lowe and Andrew Flynn believe this has been the result of a low-profile strategy followed by the government, the abandonment of a search for nuclear waste disposal sites, strategic mistakes by the anti-nuclear campaign of the 1980s and the shifting of support to a newly revived Campaign for Nuclear Disarmament in the early 1980s.[17] Ironically, nuclear power was ultimately to be confronted most effectively by the policies of the Thatcher administration itself (see below).

As of 1986–7, the level of public and governmental interest in pollution issues was not significantly greater than it had been a decade before. Since then, however, these issues have achieved a new prominence. The change has come partly as a result of the public debate arising out of Mrs Thatcher's plans for the privatization of the electricity and water supply industries. It has also come as a result of the tightening of pollution control legislation arising out of European Community decisions, which has drawn attention to the shortcomings in British legislation. Finally, there has been a new interest in international and/or global pollution problems, notably global warming and the ozone layer.

Privatization and pollution

Although barely mentioned in the 1979 Conservative election manifesto, privatization became one of the foundations of latter-day Thatcherism, and a policy copied in several other countries. Particularly during her second administration, Mrs Thatcher oversaw an extensive privatization programme that resulted in the sale to the private sector of such institutions as British Airways, British Gas, British Telecom and the British Airports Authority. The privatization of industries providing basic services was a relative latecomer to the programme; plans to privatize the water and electricity supply industries were first mooted – respectively – in 1986 and 1987, and completed in 1990. They also proved more unpopular than earlier privatization programmes; opinion polls revealed only 15 per cent in favour of water privatization, and 22 per cent in favour of electricity privatization.[18]

At first, privatization was motivated by concerns for efficiency, and a belief by Thatcherites that private enterprise could provide more efficient service than state-owned industries.[19] Over time, the emphasis shifted away from the efficiency argument towards the financial argument: selling off state-owned industries to raise money for current spending and to reduce the public sector borrowing requirement.[20] In the case of the water and electricity supply industries, the motivation was ostensibly an injection of competition. However, there was considerable doubt about whether the final structure of the privatized electricity supply industry actually promoted competition at all. In both cases, privatization also revealed an administration that had not fully considered all the economic and environmental consequences.

Plans for the privatization of the water supply industry led not only to an immediate critical response from environmental groups (leading ultimately to significant changes in the final arrangements made for privatization), but also to an unexpected and almost unprecedented level of public debate in 1988–9 about the quality of Britain's water. Many people were made aware for the first time that Britain's water quality – long thought to be good – was often worse than that in other European countries. Privatization also subjected the system of water pollution control in Britain to an unprecedented level of public scrutiny, and brought to a head efforts by the European Community dating back at least four years to persuade Britain to comply with EC water purity standards.

Efforts to control water pollution in Britain date from the Rivers Pollution Prevention Act of 1876, which was never enforced. In 1946, the Attlee government was moved to describe the state of Britain's rivers as a "scandal", and passed legislation consolidating the existing administrative system, creating 32 river boards in England and Wales. The system was changed again with the 1963 Water Resources Act, which created 29 river authorities with additional powers over conservation. A lack of funding and the difficulties of enforcing sewage standards led ultimately to the failure of this system, so that by the late 1960s the quality of water in Britain had become critical.

The Heath government in 1973 removed water from the control of local government, and created ten Regional Water Authorities (RWAs) in England and Wales, giving them responsibility over all aspects of water management, including conservation, sewerage and sewage disposal, and the control of emissions (including their own) into rivers. In 1974, the Wilson administration passed the Control of Pollution Act, a law proposed by the Heath administration which was now enthusiastically received by the opposition spokesperson on the environment, Margaret Thatcher. Among other things, the Act increased the availability to the public of information on polluters.

The original Thatcher government white paper on water privatization, issued in February 1986, proposed passing on almost all the reponsibilities of the RWAs to the new private water company. The environmental lobby had never been happy with the fact that the RWAs could regulate themselves, and protested that this arrangement was being allowed to continue. CPRE immediately embarked on a period of active involvement in the debate over privatizing both water and electricity, becoming more involved – to its own surprise – than most other environmental groups.[21] In 1986, it took legal opinion on the matter, and found that placing pollution control in the hands of private companies would be illegal under European Community law. The European Commission was alerted, and warned the British government that there was a need for an independent "competent authority" to oversee pollution control. The subsequent public debate over pollution control, combined with questions about pricing and planning, encouraged Nicholas Ridley, the environment secretary, to withdraw the proposal and postpone it until after the next election.

Meanwhile, a study by the Water Research Centre (commissioned by the Department of the Environment) was published in 1987, suggesting that river quality in Britain was better on average than that in many other EC countries. Yet most other evidence suggested that the pollution of Britain's river water, groundwater and drinking water was a serious problem. Central government budget cuts had reduced the ability of RWAs to keep water clean; inadequate control over the use of pesticides, nitrates, chlorinated solvents and sewage disposal had resulted in worsening pollution; and prosecutions of offenders had proved so rare as to provide little disincentive. The number of pollution incidents reported by the RWAs in 1987–8 was a 9.5 per cent increase over the previous year, and an increase of 86 per cent over 1980, but only 254 prosecutions of polluters were made by RWAs in 1985–6, despite nearly 20,000 incidents.[22]

In 1987, Nicholas Ridley unveiled the government's amended plans for the privatized water industry. Instead of giving pollution control responsibilities to the new private companies, the government proposed setting up a new, independent National Rivers Authority (NRA). The NRA would have regulatory powers over pollution control, and responsibility for land drainage, fisheries, conservation and recreation. CPRE was to claim most of the credit for encouraging the creation of the NRA.[23] While this new arrangement assuaged some of the fears of the environmental lobby, concern remained that the NRA would not have enough staff, resources or powers to carry out its functions effectively. In 1988, CPRE launched a water appeal aimed at raising funds to finance a new parliamentary lobbying campaign aimed at making conservation amendments to the Water Bill. A report on the environmental implications of water privatization was commissioned from Leeds University at the beginning of 1988 by CPRE, the RSPB and WWF, and copies were sent to every MP immediately before the second reading of the bill in December 1988.

The success of water privatization was further complicated in mid-1989 by the government missing the deadline to apply for a US listing for the share flotation; by fears that the costs of dealing with nitrate pollution would make privatization less attractive (nitrate pollution was particularly serious in East Anglia, and scientists at the Anglian Water Authority were threatened with criminal proceedings if they made public statements about water quality); and by a decision by the European Commission to take the British government to the European Court of Justice over failure to meet EC water quality standards.

Meanwhile, privatization of the electricity supply industry was having similarly unanticipated consequences. In this case, they were leading to a rethinking of the entire future of the British nuclear power industry. Electricity supply was the biggest of all the industries sold off by the Thatcher administration. Like the water industry, the activities of the electricity industry had long been isolated from public scrutiny. Privatization now subjected it to a rigorous examination, which revealed for the first time the real costs of nuclear power (previously buried in the accounts of a supply industry that made most of its profits from coal-fired electricity generation).

Privatization was completed in 1990, when the Central Electricity Generating Board (CEGB) was replaced by two new private companies: National Power, responsible for 70 per cent of existing CEGB power-stations, and PowerGen, responsible for the balance, and assumed to be National Power's competitor in a new power generation duopoly. The government had originally planned that National Power should have two divisions, one operating thermal plants and the other nuclear plants. When electricity privatization was considered in more depth, however, new problems were raised.

The first was the cost of nuclear power. Mrs Thatcher had been an enthusiastic proponent of nuclear power, since it seemed to offer solutions to a number of urgent problems. She believed not only that there was a strong strategic argument in favour of developing the nuclear power industry, but that it would further reduce dependence upon the coal mining industry, and that it would help reduce the production of the carbon dioxide implicated in global warming. She was using this argument as late as the summer of 1989. However, the generation of nuclear power had already proved substantially more expensive than energy generated by coal-fired power-stations. In 1987–8, the CEGB achieved a real return on its assets of just 2.4 per cent. In 1988, electricity prices were raised by 9 per cent, supposedly in an attempt to increase the profitability of electricity prior to privatization.[24]

In 1987, a report by the Nuclear Installation Inspectorate on the Bradwell Magnox power-station was published. Britain had built twenty-six Magnox reactors between 1956 and 1971, of which seven are still in use. At the time of construction, Magnox stations were expected to have a useful life of 20 to 25 years. Bradwell, having been built in 1962, was by 1987 nearing the end of its estimated lifespan. While no major problems were revealed, there were enough potential weaknesses in the power-station to prompt the government to direct the CEGB to make rapid safety improvements if Bradwell was to continue operating until 1992, as the CEGB wanted.

The report on the Bradwell station presaged a widening debate about the safety and reliability of Magnox reactors in particular, and nuclear power-stations in general, and about the costs of either maintaining or decommissioning them. The costs of repair and maintenance, coupled with doubts about their long-term safety and reliability, promised to make nuclear power-stations a major liability. The attractiveness of the electricity generation industry to potential buyers was further reduced by other concerns:

- The likelihood of public controversies over the building of three new pressurized-water reactors (PWRs). The construction of the Sizewell B PWR (which has yet to be completed) had attracted much opposition from environmental groups during the early 1980s – the public inquiry into Sizewell became the longest in British history, lasting 340 days over a two-year period.
- An impending shortage of storage space for spent fuel rods from advanced gas-cooled reactors (AGRs).
- The doubtful reliability of AGRs.
- The considerable capital cost and poor return on investment in new stations.

In July 1989, shortly after the privatization bill came to be read in the House of Lords, the plan to include Britain's seven Magnox nuclear power-stations in National Power was shelved when it was revealed that they would cost £1 to £2 billion each to decommission. This would clearly have made National Power unattractive to private investors. In November, the government announced that it was withdrawing the remaining nuclear power-stations from the sale, and abandoning plans to commission the three new PWRs. The resignation of Lord Marshall, chairman of the CEGB and then of National Power, was also announced. Long pilloried by environmentalists for his opposition to controls on acid pollution, Lord Marshall had also been blamed by Conservative MPs for misleading the government over the costs of nuclear power. (Much blame was also laid at the door of the former energy secretary, Cecil Parkinson, for miscalculating the real costs of nuclear power.)

Britain's remaining nuclear power-stations were subsequently given over to a new publicly owned company, Nuclear Electric. The first chairman of the company, John Collier, immediately went on the defensive, arguing that the costs of nuclear power had been misrepresented and misunderstood, and that it was in fact an economic alternative to fossil-fuel-powered electricity generation. Unless nuclear power can be made economic, however, there is a very real prospect that the operational costs of nuclear power-stations, now that they are no longer balanced out by the more profitable coal-fired power-stations, will ultimately lead to the abandonment of Britain's nuclear power programme in its entirety.

Given that the British government has yet to make any serious commitment to investigating new, alternative sources of energy (such as solar, wind, wave and tide generation), it now has three remaining options. Assuming that nuclear power is not proved economic, it must: (1) extend its reliance on coal-fired power-stations, at the same time taking into account that measures will have to be taken to reduce carbon dioxide emissions from those stations; (2) buy more nuclear-generated electricity from France, which meets 70 per cent of its own electricity needs with nuclear power, and already meets about 5 per cent of British needs; or (3) invest more time and money in energy conservation, an option that would please the environmental lobby. Future pressure may be brought to bear in this regard by European Community objectives on energy conservation.

Public scrutiny of the costs of nuclear power was not the only unexpected consequence of electricity privatization. Repeating the pattern used on the water privatization issue, a trio of environmental groups (this time CPRE, WWF and Friends of the Earth) commissioned a report from Sussex University on the environmental consequences of privatization.[25] The report formed the basis of a lobbying campaign by CPRE and other groups, aimed at raising concerns about the environmental protection arrangements of the new private energy companies. In partnership with the Association for the Conservation of Energy, the three groups issued a policy pamphlet entitled *Greening the Bill*. This pointed out that electricity generation produced sulphur dioxide (SO_2), nitrogen oxides (NOx), carbon dioxide (CO_2) and radioactive waste. While EC regulations would compel Britain to reduce SO_2 and NOx, nothing was yet being done about CO_2. The groups called for energy efficiency, energy conservation and target reductions in the production of pollutants.[26]

Interest group pressure ultimately helped bring about amendments to the Electricity Bill, placing a general environmental duty on the energy secretary and the new Office of Electricity Regulation (Offer). Suppliers and generators were made responsible for doing whatever they could to lessen the negative effects on natural beauty when building stations or other structures. This included drawing up environmental guidelines in consultation with the NCC and Countryside Commission. The energy secretary was also made responsible for taking environmental matters into account when considering planning applications.

It is ironic that British nuclear power, long opposed by the environmental lobby, should ultimately have been undermined not by the efforts of that lobby alone, but by the policies of the very administration which had promoted nuclear power so enthusiastically during the 1980s. If electricity generation had not been privatized, and the CEGB had been retained intact, it is quite likely that the Thatcher administration (or any subsequent Conservative administrations) would have ordered an expansion in nuclear power. While continuing to be unpopular among many environmentalists, the development of nuclear power might have squared well with any future commitments by the British government to reduce the carbon dioxide emitted by coal-fired power-stations, and implicated in global warming.

In retrospect, it is obvious that the implications of water and electricity privatization were not fully worked out by the government during the early planning stages. Mrs Thatcher uncharacteristically admitted as much herself, when she told the Conservative local government conference in March 1989 that "the subject of privatization of water has not in fact been handled well or accurately". The National Society for Clean Air felt that part, if not most, of the problem arose from the government seeking "to cure the problems of pollution without facing up to the fundamental policies which ... caused them in the first place". The Society wrote to Chris Patten in August 1989 arguing that the departments of energy and the environment lacked political direction, and calling for the creation of a statutory, independent, non-political body to advise the government on environment and pollution policy.[27]

Privatization ultimately played into the hands of the environmental lobby by helping draw public attention to the parlous state of Britain's fresh water, to the costs of nuclear energy and to the weaknesses in pollution control policy. It also took pollution control out of the hands of the water and electricity supply industries for the first time, and – thanks largely to pressures from the environmental lobby and the European Community – resulted in a substantial restructuring of the management of water and electricity supply in Britain. Provided the NRA and Offer are given sufficient powers, the new arrangements will impose the strongest controlling influence ever on the environmental aspects of water and electricity supply in Britain. However, this is likely to result in substantial increases in supply charges.

The globalization of pollution issues

Another reason underlying the increased prominence of pollution issues on the policy agenda was the growing attention paid in the late 1980s throughout the industrialized world to problems of global proportions. Notable among these were the threats posed to the ozone layer by chlorofluorocarbons, and the dangers of climate change and global warming associated with a build-up of carbon dioxide, methane and CFCs in the atmosphere. In both cases, British domestic policy – like the policies of other industrialized countries – has been influenced and determined as much as anything by negotiations among the governments of those countries, rather than by pressure from the domestic environmental lobby.

On the ozone issue, the Thatcher administration was the victim of circumstance. CFCs had first been developed in 1928, since when they had been used increasingly in aerosols, refrigeration, air-conditioning, solvents and polyurethane containers. Evidence that CFCs might harm the ozone layer was first published in 1974, and the United Nations Environment Programme established a research co-ordination committee in 1977. In March 1985, a convention was signed in Vienna by twenty countries that committed them to little beyond research and a broad agreement to control activities posing an actual or potential threat to the ozone layer.

Two months later, research was published revealing that British scientists had discovered a thinning of the ozone layer over the Antarctic. This increased the pressure for action to freeze and/or reduce CFC production, and in September 1987 an international agreement (the Montreal Protocol) was signed by the United States, the European Community and twenty-three other countries. They agreed to freeze production of CFCs by 1990, and to work towards a 30 per cent reduction by 1999. This would only have had the effect of slowing down ozone destruction, however; many scientists argued that an 85 per cent reduction was needed simply to prevent atmospheric CFC concentrations from increasing, and that a total ban was the most desirable option.

Until 1987, Britain had taken a notably obstructionist position on the CFC issue, preventing the European Community from taking a collective decision to reduce CFC production. In July 1987, however, it reversed its position, and began promoting the goal of CFC reductions. John Gribbin suggests that the policy reversal may have been the work of William Waldegrave, then junior environment minister, who was personally concerned about the ozone layer problem. He also notes a more plausable explanation: that restricting CFCs would cost the British government very little.[28]

Mrs Thatcher had begun taking a personal interest in the ozone issue, going so far as to arrange for London to host the March 1989 conference called to update the Montreal Protocol. In the preceding months, the British government took a strong position on CFC reduction, earning some rare (if qualified) praise from Friends of the Earth. The DOE's decision to press for an 85 per cent reduction in CFC production was good, FoE noted; however, it was a relatively easy position to adopt, since consumer pressure and media attention, "largely generated by FoE campaigns", had resulted in the main manufacturers and retailers of aerosols and fast food packaging announcing in 1988 their intention to rapidly phase out the use of CFCs. (Between 1986 and 1989, consumption of CFCs in Britain had been halved by replacing CFCs in aerosols with butane.) With industry already voluntarily moving away from CFC use, FoE felt that the new position of the British government required little of its own initiative.[29] Hence Mrs Thatcher could afford to take a position on the CFC issue that was closer to that of the environmental lobby, since it would cost industry and her administration relatively little.

On the issue of global warming, the debate so far has revolved more around scientific uncertainty than around political initiatives. Assuming that the link between CO_2 and global warming is confirmed and accepted by governments, reducing CO_2 will mean, among other things, taking further steps to clean emissions from power-stations and other users of fossil fuels. Mrs Thatcher spoke in general terms about the desirability of preventing global warming, but little action is likely to be taken by any industrialized country without confirmation that global warming is indeed occurring, and that the burden of making carbon dioxide reductions will be shared among the major industrialized countries.

Conclusions

Pollution issues achieved a new prominence in British politics during the late 1980s. The temptation is to assume that the environmental lobby, as the traditional source of most of the pressure for change on environmental policy, was a primary cause of this shift. However, closer examination reveals that the environmental lobby played a rather different role.

Instead of responding as usual to what it saw as deficiencies in public policy, and generating pressure for change, the lobby found itself having to respond to *government* initiatives, and being able to make use of opportunities unwittingly provided by the government to change policy. In the past, the lobby has regularly applied pressure to make polluting industries and pollution control agencies more accountable to the public, and to force a change in policy on nuclear power, but with only limited success. With privatization, the nature of British water pollution control and the true costs of nuclear power were subjected to unexpected public scrutiny and debate, providing the lobby with unexpected opportunities to promote real changes in policy. The most ironic aspect of the subsequent policy changes was the fact that the ardently deregulatory Thatcher administration found itself compelled, as a consequence of its own policies, to actually *extend* regulation over water pollution control, and to make public the uneconomic costs of nuclear power. The lobby also used the opportunity provided by changes in domestic legislation arising out of European Community requirements to draw attention to shortcomings in Thatcherite proposals for restructuring institutions and laws relating to pollution control.

With regard to changes arising out of international negotiations to reduce sulphur dioxide, nitrogen oxides, CFCs and carbon dioxide, however, the environmental lobby played a relatively limited role. Again unexpectedly, pressures from outside Britain – from other European governments and the United States – ultimately proved more effective in bringing about domestic policy changes.

6. The New Green Society

In September 1988, a book entitled *The Green Consumer Guide* was published in Britain, written by John Elkington and Julia Hailes. The book was a practical guide for consumers, describing the links between consumer lifestyle and environmental problems, analysing the environmental effects of a wide range of consumer products, and giving advice on how consumers could change their lifestyle so that it was more environmentally sustainable. It was published to coincide with Britain's first Green Consumer Week. Its publication also coincided (fortuitously) with Mrs Thatcher's references to the environment in her speeches to the Royal Society (September) and the Conservative Party conference (October).

In the following seven months, the *Guide* went through eleven impressions. It featured in the *Sunday Times* bestseller list for thirty-five weeks. Within a year, it had sold 350,000 copies. In September 1989 a Green Shopping Day was held in conjunction with the *Guide*, involving companies, environmental groups and individual consumers. In 1990, nine foreign versions of the *Guide* were published, including an American edition. These were all rewritten to meet the needs of consumers in those countries. Australian and Canadian versions sold 100,000 copies within two months of publication. A British sequel to the *Guide*, *The Green Consumer's Supermarket Guide* (a practical handbook based on a questionnaire survey undertaken among the major British supermarket groups and several hundred manufacturers), sold 100,000 copies within months of publication, and was followed by a young person's guide.

The Green Consumer Guide became one of the bestselling environmental books ever. It may yet prove to have an influence on public thinking that parallels (even supersedes) the influence of *Silent Spring* by Rachel Carson. Throughout 1989, "green consumerism" was one of the most fashionable and most widely publicized and discussed concepts in British public life. A MORI poll in June 1989 revealed that more than 18 million people, nearly half the adult population of Britain, considered themselves environmentally conscious shoppers; this was an increase of 121 per cent over the previous year. It further found that 42 per cent of people questioned met the MORI definition of a "green consumer": someone who had made at least one purchase in the previous twelve months where one product was selected over another because of its environmentally conscious packaging, formulation or advertising. In 1988, only 19 per cent of consumers could be so defined.[1] Suddenly, it seemed that it was chic to be green. Yet the permanence and longterm effect of green consumerism were already being questioned by the end of 1989. A MORI poll in December revealed that there had been no increase in the number of green consumers, and some interpreted this as the beginning of a decline in green consumerism. However, the lack of further growth may simply have been because green consumerism had already reached saturation point earlier in the year.

Coincident with the growth of green consumerism, the British Green Party attracted growing support during the late 1980s. Before 1989, it had never won more than 1.5 per cent of the vote at general elections, or 5.9 per cent of the vote at local elections.[2] At the June 1989 European Parliament elections, it surprised almost everyone, including itself, by winning 15 per cent of the vote, more than twice the combined share of the Liberal Democrats and the Social Democrats. This was not only by far the best performance in its seventeen-year history, but the best performance of any green party anywhere in Europe. While the result must be treated with some caution (see below), and did not result in British Greens winning any seats in Strasbourg, it nevertheless prompted much discussion about the relevance of green ideology to Thatcherite Britain, and posed some interesting questions about the changing nature of British environmentalism. It also made many more people take notice of green politics. At least during 1989, the green consumer movement – combined with the increased popularity of the Green Party – led to a rethinking about the relationship between consumerism, Thatcherism and the environmental lobby. The rethinking occurred largely irrespective of age or region, although most green consumers and voters alike tended to be middle class.

The rise of green consumerism

As with so many ideas in modern environmentalism, the concept of a link between consumer demand and environmental degradation is not new. The links between capitalism and consumption were analysed in 1958 by John Kenneth Galbraith in his book *The Affluent Society*, which discussed the excessive demand and superfluous production of postwar society.[3] At the height of the New Environmentalism of the early 1970s, several books were published which – like *The Green Consumer Guide* – warned of the dangers of excessive consumption, and tried to show how individuals were responsible for environmental problems.[4] In 1985, *The User's Guide to the Environment*[5] sold barely 2,000 copies, although it made many of the arguments later dealt with in more depth by Elkington and Hailes. There was clearly only limited public interest in green consumerism in 1985.

However, consumer interest in environmental matters changed markedly in the second half of the decade. As in the United States, the 1980s in Britain saw a new level of public interest in personal health and fitness. More people also began paying more attention to the quality of their diet, and there was a growing demand for food and drink that were free of artificial additives, fat and cholesterol. Organic food and drink (from crops grown without the use of artificial fertilizers and pesticides, and sold without artificial additives) became more popular, as reflected, for example, in support for such organizations as the Campaign for Real Ale (CAMRA) and the Campaign for Real Bread (CAMREB). By 1990, Safeway was finding that it could not meet the demand for organic food in its supermarkets. It predicted that the market for organic foods (which accounted for 4 per cent of Safeway's fresh fruit and vegetable sales) could triple by 1993.[6]

Vegetarianism also became more popular during the late 1980s, and there was increased demand for healthier and more natural products (such as decaffeinated drinks, organic wine, unsweetened fruit and fruit juices, and meat from animals raised on farms that did not use growth-inducing hormones). There was also more demand for "clear-conscience" products (such as free range eggs, tuna caught without the finely woven nets that result in the incidental deaths of dolphins, and cosmetics that were not tested on animals). An early indication of this heightened consumer sensitivity for "quality of life" issues was the enormous success of a bland and factual paperback book entitled *E for Additives* by Maurice Hanssen. First published in 1987, the book was a practical explanation of the additives found in many British foods (denoted by a number beginning in an E). In its first edition alone it sold 500,000 copies.

By the second half of the 1980s, there was obviously a growing market for sensitive consumerism. The idea for *The Green Consumer Guide* grew out of a series of discussions that John Elkington held with public relations and advertising companies in the mid-1980s. They told him of the growing public interest in green consumerism, which they ascribed to changes in industry leading up to the removal of internal trading barriers in the European Community in 1992.[7] Elkington had already spent many years working on environmental issues, including two years as managing director of Environmental Data Services (ENDS). ENDS was founded in the early 1970s by Max Nicholson, one of Britain's most respected environmentalists (among many other things, he was the former director of the Nature Conservancy Council, and cofounder of WWF and the British Trust for Conservation

Volunteers). Nicholson had founded ENDS to provide objective reports to industry on the environmental impact of industrial and commercial activities. Nicholson recalls that in its early years, ENDS had found it difficult to survive because of a lack of interest on the part of industry.[8]

In 1987, together with Julia Hailes and Tom Burke, Elkington founded SustainAbility, a private company looking for new ways to promote environmentally sustainable economic growth. It did this through providing consultancy services such as environmental audits, advice on existing products and help with environmental policy and strategy formation. The company's first major project was the publication of *Green Pages*, a guide to opportunities in the environmental field for business, investment and employment.[9] Publication of *Green Pages* was followed by *The Green Consumer Guide* and the publication in September 1989 of *The Green Consumer Supermarket Guide*.

"We set up SustainAbility at a time that caught the wave of a new generation of consumers that had grown up knowing more and more about the damage being inflicted on the environment," Elkington recalls. "There's nothing new in the idea that consumer decisions can influence the world we live in, but there is in the idea that the power of consumerism can be harnessed to make industry more environmentally responsible."[10]

Thanks to this new interest in green consumerism, it had become common by the end of 1989 for companies to boast their green credentials, and to use the environment as a positive selling point. Among the products promoted as green were unleaded petrol (Shell and Esso), batteries (Panasonic and Varta), chlorine-free disposable nappies (Peaudouce and Proctor & Gamble), "environmentally friendly" cars (Volkswagen, Audi and Vauxhall), washing machines, dishwashers and refrigerators (AEG) and supermarket chains (Tesco and the Co-op). A number of new companies were also set up specifically to meet the demand for environmentally friendly products. One of these was Ecover, a company which sells environmentally friendly cleaning products. Although founded in 1979, it only achieved real prominence in Britain in 1989.

Also in 1989, The Ark was launched amid considerable publicity, partly to function as a campaigning pressure group in the mould of most other environmental groups, but also to market environmentally sound consumer products. It had a mixed reception from existing groups, some of which claimed that there was no room for new organizations focusing on middle class consumers. The consumer element in The Ark's constitution exemplified the importance, at least in early 1989, of green consumerism to the environmental lobby. The Ark marketed a successful range of biodegradable cleaning products, and had plans for a nationwide chain of fastfood vegetable burgers.

Where did green consumerism come from? It is still too early to know for sure, but ironically it is arguable that the ground for green consumerism was at least partly prepared by Thatcherism. The consumer society in Britain (as elsewhere in Western Europe) had grown steadily since the 1950s. Mrs Thatcher extended this by promoting increased domestic production and consumption, by making much of her admiration for entrepreneurs, and by encouraging British industry to become more competitive, and more responsive to the needs of its customers. The irony of the coalescence of Thatcherite enterprise and green consumerism is nowhere better exemplified than in the success of The Body Shop International.

The Body Shop was founded in 1976 by Anita Roddick, with the objective of selling environmentally and ethically acceptable alternatives to many of the personal care products sold by conventional retailers. Among other things, it formulates its products only from natural ingredients, refuses to sell products whose ingredients have been tested on animals in the preceding five years, uses minimal packaging for its products, and uses its shop windows to promote environmental and community issues. Roddick says that she

> never set out to "capture" Green Consumers. They didn't exist, or certainly not by that name, when I started The Body Shop in 1976. But their power is steadily growing. The new type of

> consumer can be found everywhere, in pin-striped suits, white coats or boiler-suits.[11]

The Body Shop has been a very successful business venture, and its success has been built partly on Mrs Thatcher's enterprise culture, and partly on the rise of green consumer concerns. In 1987, it was named Company of the Year in the annual Business Enterprise Awards. By 1988, it had a turnover of nearly £30 million, and had almost 300 branches in thirty-one countries.

The success of *The Green Consumer Guide* – and the broader rise of the green consumer movement – may have been both a consequence of *and* a reaction to the Thatcherite enterprise culture. While the enterprise culture encouraged entrepreneurs, it also may have caused a reaction on the part of consumers concerned about the uncaring accumulation of money by business. Ivor Crewe argues that the broad aims of economic and social transformation contained in Thatcherism have not been translated into changes in individual attitudes. Most people apparently still put caring before wealth creation. "There has been no Thatcherite transformation of attitudes or behaviour among the British public," Crewe argues. "If anything, the British have edged further away from Thatcherite positions as the decade has progressed."[12] A MORI poll in June 1988 found that 75 per cent of people thought that the creation of wealth was more important than caring for others in Thatcherite Britain, and that 73 per cent felt that people were permitted to make and keep as much money as they could. At the same time, 49 per cent preferred a "mainly socialist society", compared to 43 per cent who preferred a "mainly capitalist society", and 79 per cent preferred a society in which caring for others was more highly rewarded than the creation of wealth.[13]

Lower tax rates, privatization and the enterprise culture have combined to increase the number of shareholders in Britain, to increase the number of homeowners (particularly with the sale of council housing), to generate greater personal mobility and to increase the availability of disposable income. They have also combined to give more people a more direct stake in industrial, agricultural and economic policy. There has also been an expansion of the middle class, amd a growth in generation and accumulation of "new money", especially in the South-East. Yet public opinion would seem to indicate a rejection of Thatcherite enterprise at the expense of the quality of life; in other words, it reveals a populace that is concerned about the quality of life, and concerned that Thatcherite capitalism has promoted a lack of concern for such quality. Hence green consumerism might be interpreted as a reaction to the values of "low conscience" free enterprise, and to a concern that Thatcher's Britain has created new wealth as never before, but with little care for the welfare of the consumer or the environment.

Whatever the motives behind green consumerism, the rise in demand for green products was so rapid in 1988 and 1989 that there was much media discussion in the summer and autumn of 1989 about the lack of a sound method of labelling "green" products. A labelling system would distinguish genuine products from those making fraudulent claims in order to attract green consumer business. In July 1989, a joint study group was convened by the Department of the Environment and the Department of Trade and Industry to examine the idea of a green label. A DOE discussion paper was issued in August, expressing the need for reliable, independent standards, but arguing that they should be voluntary, flexible and simple, and – so as not to create a new barrier to the European Single Market – part of an EC-wide standard rather than the latest in a growing series of national standards. (Germany had introduced a labelling scheme in 1978, and France and the Netherlands were also considering schemes during 1989.) Nearly a year later, the DOE was able only to promise a voluntary labelling system by the end of 1991. Friends of the Earth anticipated some of these delays in September 1989 by instituting an award for the "Green Con of the Year", designed to draw attention to companies fraudulently claiming that their products were environmentally sound.

As green consumerism grew, so there was a growth in the

number of environmental consultancies and in the incidence of environmental auditing, a service offered to companies concerned with ensuring that they were complying with environmental legislation. According to Environmental Data Services (itself a consultancy), the number of consultancies almost doubled in 1988–90, from 125 to nearly 250. The World Wide Fund for Nature, which relies heavily on corporate sponsors (see below), announced that it was considering insisting that companies wanting to use the WWF panda logo on their products should undergo environmental audits.[14]

Environmental groups and the green consumer

John Elkington believes that environmental groups had only limited influence on the creation of the green consumer revolution: "Environmental groups were rather left behind and surprised by the green consumer wave; about the only exception was FoE's best-selling booklet[15] on aerosols."[16]

Tom Burke disagrees, arguing that environmental groups were responsible for raising consciousness to the point where the green consumer movement could emerge: "Environmental groups created the green consumer revolution; they just didn't know what they were doing." He believes that they did raise consciousness, and while there is no "winning post" to which environmentalists are headed, environmental groups have won

> in the sense of raising the environment to the point where it is a major item on the political agenda. We've won that. This is a *major* step forward, and the culmination of twenty years' work. Public awareness is one thing – now we're beginning to see changes in lifestyles.[17]

Indeed, many environmental groups had tried to promote consumer awareness and harness the support of consumers well before the publication of *The Green Consumer Guide*. Some examples:

- Environmental groups drew attention during the 1980s to the fact that fast-food chains such as McDonalds and Burger King were implicated in tropical deforestation, since they used beef raised on Latin American farms that had been established on land converted from virgin tropical rain forest. They also drew attention to the fact that many fast-food chains used packaging containing CFCs.
- The anti-cruelty lobby has for many years campaigned against the testing of cosmetics and pharmaceuticals on animals. In particular, the British Union for the Abolition of Vivisection (BUAV) and the Royal Society for the Prevention of Cruelty to Animals (RSPCA) have been active in drawing attention to "cruelty-free" companies.
- In 1987, Greenpeace orchestrated a boycott of fish fingers containing Icelandic fish in order to put pressure on Iceland to cease whaling.
- Groups such as Greenpeace and Lynx (an offshoot of Greenpeace) have for many years campaigned against the use of furs, resulting in a noticeable reduction in the fashionability of – and demand for – fur coats.

Not only did the environmental lobby arguably create the foundation for a broader interest in green consumerism, but Elkington and Burke (given their background in environmental groups) were themselves at least partly products of the environmental lobby.

Whatever the role of environmental groups in helping create the green consumer movement, the advent of this movement has demanded new responses and new tactics on the part of the environmental lobby. Elkington believes that "environmentalists have got to recognize that they have to get involved in marketing – we've got to sell the environment to people. Groups are going to have to become service-oriented businesses, actually providing people with the services they want."[18] This view is supported by Burke:

> Environmentalists are bemused about the 20 to 30 per cent growth in their membership rates, and wondering what they should think about the green consumer. Members of groups are buying someone

> to go out and fight for the environment for them. Groups have responded well to this demand.[19]

Chris Tydeman of WWF notes an "overnight switch" in the way companies have dealt with the Fund: "They want to be seen to be green, and they want to get involved in initiatives and promotions with environmental groups that would improve their green credentials."[20] There has also been a response from groups, some of which have already changed their tactics. Jonathon Porritt relates one particularly notable change in the methods of Friends of the Earth since 1987, from campaigning and working *against* industry to working increasingly *with* industry.

He recalls that on the issue of chlorofluorocarbons (CFCs), implicated in damage to the Earth's ozone layer, FoE was initially confrontational, threatening a boycott against the British Aerosol Manufacturers' Association. With the construction industry, FoE's tactics were very different.

> We realized that most of the construction companies didn't know about the effects of CFC use, so we commissioned Salford University to write a report on CFC use in the construction industry. The research took nine months, and they came up with a very technical report which was well received by the industry; they said we had given them the tools whereby they could begin making the changes.[21]

Porritt suggests that Friends of the Earth has had to develop this service-oriented approach because there is now much more public awareness of environmental problems, and public and industry alike are now increasingly interested in *responding* to problems with concrete action, rather than simply learning about the existence of problems. "In the old days," he recalls,

> FoE spent a lot of time beating at doors because people didn't want to let us in. We had to work hard to get the attention of ministers, for example. Now we just have to nudge the door, it opens wide, and we fall flat on our faces, not really knowing what to do when we get there. We get letters every week now from industries and companies asking for recommendations on courses of action.[22]

For Friends of the Earth, this has meant a new emphasis on practical, advice-based campaigning rather than criticism and confrontation. Instead of criticizing companies for being environmentally destructive, Friends of the Earth believes it must give them the practical means by which they can improve and change their practices. The strategy of providing technical information to industry came about almost accidentally. In 1986, a Friends of the Earth strategy meeting decided to spend more money on commissioning authoritative research reports for parliamentary committees. By extension, it was also decided to make this information availible to industry and professionals. "Luckily we were just ahead of the game by about a year," recalls Porritt.[23]

Many environmental groups have had a long record of associating themselves with companies promoting an interest in environmental issues, usually to the benefit of both parties. Philip Lowe recalls that, during the research for his survey of environmental groups in the early 1980s,[24] he noticed that government and industrial sponsorship of environmental groups was growing in aggregate terms. Some groups – particularly more conservative groups and those oriented towards practical conservation work, rather than campaigning – were very heavily dependent on these sources of funds. Since then, even groups which at the time said they would not accept that kind of sponsorship (such as CPRE and Friends of the Earth) have accepted more corporate sponsorship. This, he argues, reflects the degree to which they have become more "reputable" and are adjusting their strategies.[25]

Groups such as the World Wide Fund for Nature and the National Trust were already very much involved in such promotions, and have simply increased the number of promotions during the 1980s. For WWF, one of the biggest of these was the "Guardians of the Countryside" campaign, a joint venture with H. J. Heinz, involving a budget of £1 million. Agreements were also reached between WWF and tour companies such as Sun Med Holidays, Thomson Holidays and Twickers World, where the companies gave their clients information on how to avoid degrading the environment during their vacation, or where the companies made a small donation to WWF for each holiday sold. In the same vein, WWF has for some years run a campaign to discourage visitors to Spain from having their photographs taken with chimpanzees owned by beach photographers (for every chimpanzee so used, at least ten are estimated to die during the capture and transportation).

For WWF in particular, corporate sponsorship remains an important source of funding, accounting for 17–20 per cent of total WWF income. In 1981, the Fund raised just over £500,000 from corporate sponsors. In 1985, that figure had increased to £800,000. In the eighteen months to June 1989, companies gave £3.6 million to WWF. "The environment is rapidly catching up with sports and the arts as a commercially attractive form of sponsorship," WWF noted in a 1989 report. "Although relationships with companies can be altruistic, many corporate sponsors now want to be seen to be benefiting the environment." WWF policy is to encourage this kind of sponsorship, while at the same time influencing corporate environmental policies. The Fund's success has been such that it was commissioned by the Department of the Environment to act as a broker for the government, encouraging companies to fund other conservation groups in Britain.[26]

Philip Lowe believes that the change in attitude by industry has much to do with corporate strategies, particularly those of business interests close to the consumption end of the process. He argues that large corporate concerns have become very conscious of their public images.

> They learned gradually over a fifteen- to twenty-year period just how easily a well-devised corporate image can become unstuck by a well-aimed environmental campaign. At the consumer end there were some specific elements that helped, such as the upturn in the business cycle and shifting patterns of consumption. The four biggest supermarket retailers control about 75 per cent of retail turnover – to maintain this, they have to project a good image.[27]

Elkington argues that "the pursuit of environmental excellence is no longer an option for industry; it is a precondition for business success". He quotes the chairman of Shell UK as noting that "no business has a secure future unless it is environmentally acceptable".[28]

Provided green consumerism is not simply another consumer fad, changes in consumer lifestyle may ultimately prove the most significant outcome of the environmental movement of the 1980s. As long as responsibility for environmental protection was seen to be the preserve of the environmental lobby and government agencies, and as long as the responsibility for environmental destruction and mismanagement was seen to lie with government, industry and agriculture, supporters of the environmental lobby would have felt removed from the issue. During the late 1970s and early 1980s, it was common for those concerned about the environment to assume that it was an issue that could only be addressed by government and industry, and to believe that the individual could do little that was constructive beyond supporting the work of environmental groups.

With the emergence of green consumerism, however, not only has the individual been given a much clearer idea of the relationship between human activity and environmental destruction (and hence a more direct stake in promoting environmental protection), but no longer does the environmental lobby constitute the only significant channel through which the individual can express his or her concerns about environmental destruction. Leo Tolstoy's admonition comes to mind: "Everybody thinks of changing humanity and nobody thinks of changing himself." Green consumerism has made more people think about the role of the individual in environmental destruction, and has brought about a significant change in the way individuals relate to the environment. This has ultimately altered the nature of the whole environmental debate.

Perhaps related to this, it may be that we are now witnessing the beginning of some fundamental changes in the way individuals relate to the political process, in Britain as elsewhere in Europe. Green consumerism may be part of the criticism of "conventional" economic and political choices and structures advocated by Greens. For the Greens, capitalism and socialism in all their varieties are fundamentally unable to build sustainable societies. Western Europe (and, latterly, Eastern Europe) has witnessed growing support for alternative green policies, a trend to which Britain has not been immune. If green consumerism teaches individuals more about their place in the world, and about the consequences of a non-caring attitude to their environment, then it will have also gone some way towards promoting the kind of thinking that comprises green politics.

Green politics in Britain

The successes of the (West) German Green Party during the 1980s tended to divert attention from other green parties inside and outside Europe. For example, very few people are aware that the world's first green party (the Values Party) was founded in New Zealand in 1972. Similarly, it is often forgotten that the first country to send green delegates to a national legislature was Switzerland. Swiss greens won two seats in the Swiss parliament in 1979, four years before the West German greens first won seats in the Bundestag. Greens have gone on to become active in fifteen West European countries, and to win seats in eight West European legislatures and the European Parliament. The East European democracy movement of 1989–90 also saw the emergence of green political groups in Eastern Europe and the USSR; Romanian greens won seats in Romania's first free elections in 1990.

Similarly, it is often forgotten that Europe's oldest green party is the British Green Party. Founded under the name People in 1973, it contested its first general election in 1974. In 1975, it changed its name to the Ecology Party, and as such won 1.5 per cent of the vote in the 1979 general election, but only 1 per cent in the 1983 election. In 1985 it was renamed the Green Party. Although it won 5.9 per cent of the vote in the local elections in 1987, at the general election in that year it polled only 1.4 per cent.[29] Despite this, support for the Greens began to grow after 1987, and by early 1989 the party had attracted 11,000 members. At the June 1989 European Parliament elections, the Greens won 2.29 million votes, a 15 per cent share of the British vote. This was the best return won by a green party anywhere, and more than twice the vote anticipated by the party. But for Britain's winner-take-all electoral system, the Greens might have won twelve seats in the European Parliament. In the event, they won no seats. As of June 1989, they had only one county councillor, 11 district councillors and 90 parish councillors.

The Greens' 15 per cent share in the European elections must be treated with some caution. First, only one-third of eligible British voters turned out for the European vote, and it is likely that turnout among Green supporters was higher than average because of the greater sense of commitment and motivation among greens, and the relative apathy and/or over-confidence of Conservative and Labour voters. Opinion polls from June 1989 regularly placed the Greens at anywhere between 3 and 8 per cent, a figure that was probably more accurately reflective of their true level of support.

Secondly, it is likely that much of the vote for the Greens was a protest vote by disaffected Conservative and Labour supporters, who would be less likely to vote Green in a general election. Certainly the summer of 1989 saw much public discussion about the nature of Mrs Thatcher's leadership, and criticism of her leadership style, and of some of her policies, notably those relating to Europe. Philip Lowe is sceptical about the long-term future of the Greens: "The European elections were an opportunity for people to vote with their heart rather than their wallet. That won't be repeated at a general election, and meanwhile the major parties will try to steal their ideas."[30]

Whatever happens to Green Party support in the future, their remarkable showing in the 1989 European elections brought them from relative obscurity to considerable prominence. Had they won seats in the European Parliament, or were they able to turn their support in Britain into seats in the House of Commons (with 7 per cent of the vote, a system of proportional representation would earn them forty-five seats), they would certainly be taken more seriously as a new force in British politics. Their 1989 successes, however, took them by surprise. Although these successes brought new public interest in green politics in Britain in its wake, the scrutiny to which the Greens were subjected raised some real doubts about their goals and their abilities.

Green politics is not simply about the environment. It is ultimately about a fundamental reordering of conventional political and economic systems, advocating grass-roots democracy, local community government, human-scale technology and institutions, social equality, sustainable development, self-reliance and an holistic worldview that encourages individuals to understand their place in the world. Among other things, Greens are opposed to single leaders, preferring group leadership or a rotating leadership. Journalists interested in assessing the Greens after the European elections frequently found themselves unable to identify Green spokespeople. In the early 1980s, Jonathon Porritt was considered the primary public voice and face of the Greens. Sara Parkin and Jean Lambert subsequently became prominent representatives of the Greens, but journalists and voters alike were denied an individual Green leader. Unless journalists and voters can change their expectations of political parties, this may ultimately prove one of the downfalls of the British Greens.

Because green politics is much more than environmental politics, it does not follow that there should be much overlap between the Greens and the environmental lobby. Nor indeed is there. There is much evidence that many environmentalists have shunned the Greens, and certainly there have been few formal or informal links between the party and the environmental lobby. Parkin quotes an unpublished 1984 study suggesting much overlap between the membership of the Green Party and environmental groups, but the overlap was mainly limited to members of more radical groups, such as Friends of the Earth, Greenpeace and the Campaign for Nuclear Disarmament (the latter could only marginally be defined as an environmental group anyway).[31]

In his more recent research into the British Green Party, Philip Lowe has found very limited overlap in membership between greens and environmentalists. He sees the primary explanation as lying in the relatively greater radicalism of the Greens.[32] There is also probably still much doubt about Green

Party policies; their June 1989 successes not only found the Greens without a clearly identifiable set of leaders, but caught them without a comprehensive set of policies. Many of those policies which *had* been agreed did not always meld with the views of moderate environmentalists. The views of Tom Burke, director of the Green Alliance, who did not vote Green in the 1989 European elections, may reflect some of the doubts. "I think if [Green Party] policies were implemented it would actually be bad for the environment. Ending economic growth would lead to a decline in the environment, and leaving NATO would remove the security we need to improve it."[33]

Not only are there fundamental philosophical differences between greens and moderate environmentalists, but irrespective of the policies of a particular party, interest groups in Britain do not normally associate formally with political parties (the ties between trade unions and the Labour Party excepted). Philip Lowe believes that the environmental lobby and the Green Party sit very uneasily together. He senses that many environmental groups are embarrassed by the growth of the Greens. Because this growth begins to politicize the environment, groups find it difficult to maintain an apolitical stance. "The way they've been able to establish their influence in British society is with an apolitical strategy," he argues.

> There are big risks in throwing in your hand with any particular political party, especially a small one. You risk losing influence with the civil service if you're seen as too partisan, and you gamble all on the unlikely possibility of a future Green government.[34]

Martin Jacques, editor of *Marxism Today*, is more sanguine about the importance of the Greens, and feels that the green vote in the European elections was enormously significant. "An era is drawing to an end," he argued in 1989. He felt that Thatcherism had lost some of its appeal and much of its novelty, and that the Green vote demonstrated that there was now

> a new, radical force in the land, representing a new body of ideas and a different set of priorities. Almost overnight, it would seem,

> the radicalism of the radical right has been displaced – by a movement whose values differ markedly from those of Thatcherism.

He argues that the movement believes in the market, but also

> asserts the need for collective action by the state and supranational bodies such as the European Community. . . . Here we are not speaking simply, or even mainly, of the Green Party, but the new green aspiration in society; if you like, the green movement in its widest sense.[35]

The success of the British Greens at the European elections was sufficient – perhaps predictably – to draw responses from both the major parties. The Conservative response, which was surely motivated by some concern about the extent of Green Party successes, was led by environment secretary Nicholas Ridley, who argued that the Conservatives were the real party of conservation: "The Greens got their votes because of their name, not their policies. Once people recognize that they stand for one-sided disarmament and lower standards of living, their attraction will quickly pall."[36] In a July 1989 speech to the Association of Metropolitan Authorities in Newcastle, Ridley described the Green platform as "unscientific rubbish, based on myths, prejudices and ignorance". More broadly, he accused the Green Party and the environmental lobby of providing "very grievous disinformation".

The former MP Robert Kilroy-Silk was even less guarded in his response, which exemplified the rather uninformed and selective view of Green policies that prevails among their more conservative detractors. He suggested that the party would not survive for very long as a serious force in British politics, that it would never rival the established parties (ironically, he included the SDP among that august group, three months before its demise), and argued that "the type of pious, self-righteous, intolerant, authoritarianism of the single-issue true believer that the Greens now represent is not something, thank God, that has ever found fertile ground in the essentially pragmatic soil of British politics". He described Greens as people who "dressed in strange clothes, eat peculiar food, and want us all to live in backward rural communities". More objectively, Kilroy-Silk felt the Greens would not survive because the established parties would fill the gap in the "political market" by stealing "the more sensible Green policies". Only the established parties could make a reality of green policies, he argued, which was reason enough why every committed environmentalist (Greens included) would vote, when it counted in a general election, for one of the major parties. For the time being, he argued, the Greens were no more than a "high-profile pressure group".[37]

The major parties had already begun responding to the new popularity of green issues before the 1989 European elections. The creation of the Tory Green Initiative in 1988 was accompanied by the reconstitution of the Liberal Ecology Group as the Green Democrats. For its part, Labour decided to build a network of sympathizers inside environmental groups to advise the party on how to build its green credentials. Neil Kinnock argued that voters would scrutinize Green policies more carefully in a general election; "Those concerned about the environment are more likely to see action taken by the Labour party in government than a Green party in permanent opposition."[38]

Meanwhile, many Greens themselves are less concerned with the party winning power than with the party's core values being accepted by the major parties and by society at large. One of the party's national speakers is Jean Lambert, who said after the European elections that the Greens would not run away from government if the chance arose. "But if any other party took over our policies completely, rather than adding superficial pieces of greenery, I would be equally delighted."[39]

Conclusions

During 1988 and 1989, a fundamental and potentially far-reaching change occurred in public attitudes towards environmental issues in Britain. In a relatively marked departure from previous practice, it became common and even stylish for consumers to consider the ethical and environmental consequences of their lifestyles. There was, in effect, a green consumer revolution. Allied to this, there was in 1989 a notable growth in support for the Green Party.

It is still too early to be sure about the causes and effects of these changes. Certainly Mrs Thatcher's autumn 1988 speeches must have had considerable influence on government and public attitudes. The Thatcherite enterprise culture had also wrought changes in attitudes towards production and consumption; running parallel with the promotion of competitiveness and increased productivity, there was something of a backlash in the form of greater concern by consumers for quality of life issues. Doubts about the quality of agricultural produce and drinking water may have combined with questions about the ethics of business and industry and the continued rise of the British middle class to create a more socially and environmentally concerned consumer.

At the same time, the cumulative influence of the environmental lobby cannot be ignored. Environmental groups had worked hard over previous decades to influence public and political opinion; the changes of 1988–9 could equally be seen as the fruition of the efforts of environmental groups over many years. Whether or not the green consumer revolution and the new support for the Greens represent a permanent change in public attitudes remains to be seen. If it does, then it promises permanently to change the attitude of British governments and political parties towards environmental issues.

7. The Environment and the European Community

During the 1980s, a growing proportion of British environmental policy was made as a result of new legislation required by European Community decisions. This was particularly the case with air and water pollution, toxic wastes and problems affecting the North Sea. Community decisions also had an important effect on countryside and wildlife issues: the Common Agricultural Policy was behind much of the controversy surrounding British countryside policy, the Community directive on wild birds prompted the passage of the 1981 Wildlife and Countryside Act, and a proposed directive on the protection of natural and semi-natural habitats encouraged more discussion in the late 1980s about countryside issues.

The European Community (EC) is the only international organization in the world with the power to agree environmental policies binding on its member states. It has been at the heart of the most concerted programme being undertaken anywhere in the world to replace national environmental controls with international regulation. As more has been understood about the nature of transnational environmental problems (such as pollution), and the importance of managing common pool resources (such as fisheries and the air), so the importance of international organizations and international law has become more obvious. No organization anywhere has yet achieved anything approaching the level of change promoted by the EC.

The impact of the EC is all the more suprising considering that environmental policy was a relative latecomer to the Community policy agenda. The environment was first addressed in a 1973 Programme of Action, and subsequently developed in three additional programmes agreed in 1977, 1982 and 1987. The main goal of the programmes has been to harmonize environmental regulation and to make sure that different national standards and regulatory procedures do not interfere with free trade and business competition. Although the EC began considering environmental programmes in 1973, it was not until 1986 and the passage of the Single European Act that environmental policy was given constitutional status. Article 25 of the Act states that the Community will take action on the environment where the objectives "can be attained better at the Community level than at the level of the individual Member States". As preparations for economic integration in 1992 gathered pace in the late 1980s, so did the programme of harmonizing environmental regulation. This in turn brought about substantial changes in the structure of British environmental regulation, and fundamentally altered the role of environmental groups in the policy process.

The direct administration of environmental policies is left to member states themselves, but the Community has five legislative tools available to it: Regulations, Directives, Decisions, Recommendations and Opinions. While the European Commission would prefer to introduce pollution control regulations directly into the domestic laws of each member state, in practice it relies on Directives, the terms of which must be incorporated into domestic law before they become effective.[1] Directives are binding in terms of the goals they set, but it is up to individual member states to decide how they meet those goals. Several environmental Directives were agreed during the 1970s and 1980s. Among the most important:

- sulphur content of gas oil (light fuel oil) (adopted 1975);
- lead in petrol (1978 and 1985);
- sulphur dioxide and suspended particulates (smoke) (1980);
- lead in air (1982);
- emission of pollutants from industrial plants (1984);
- large combustion plants (1987);

- nitrogen dioxide (1985);
- several on vehicle exhaust emissions introduced since 1974.

The impact of the Community on environmental policy only really became evident in the late 1980s. In 1980, Nigel Haigh, director of the London office of the Institute for European Environmental Policy, "shared a view widely held – and certainly held within the Department of the Environment – that Community environmental policy had had little or no effect on Britain".[2] By 1984, he was writing that

> with the benefit of hindsight it can now be seen that the passing by the British Parliament of the European Communities Act 1972 was the significant step that has changed the way an important part of British environmental policy is now thought about, is enunciated and ultimately is even put into practice.[3]

In 1986, Haigh noted that environmental policy could be counted as "one of the quiet success stories of the Community".[4] By 1990, Haigh felt he could drop the adjective "quiet".[5]

As well as having a "crucial role" in changing British policy on acid pollution (see below), Haigh feels that the EC was a decisive influence on changes in British policy on reducing damage to the ozone layer. He argues that the Community gave environment minister William Waldegrave the excuse he needed to persuade ICI (a major manufacturer of CFCs) and the Department of Trade and Industry to agree to action.

> If the issue had been fought out internally, without the input of the EC and the fact that the UK, France and West Germany were individual signatories to the Vienna Convention, then Britain's negotiating position would have advanced in a different way, and we would have come under pressure from the Americans. Because there was a trial run in the EC Council, Waldegrave had the pressure put on him, and was able to come back to Britain arguing that action was needed. Hence Britain was persuaded to agree first to a 20 per cent reduction in CFC production and then to a 50 per cent reduction.[6]

Philip Lowe and Andrew Flynn are less certain about the influence of EC policy on domestic British policy. They argue that the concern of the British government with making sure that proposed Community legislation is capable of being implemented has led to such close scrutiny and modification that

> most Community directives have had no more than incremental effects on the development of domestic environmental policy. Thus, although substantial parts of the two most important pieces of British environmental legislation of the past fifteen years – the 1974 Control of Pollution Act and the 1981 Wildlife and Countryside Act – were crucially shaped by Community directives, most directives could be implemented under existing law.[7]

If there is some question about the influence of EC policy on British policy, there is no doubting that membership of the Community has opened up new opportunities to British environmental groups, which have become much more active in helping design and monitor the application of EC legislation. There have been several reasons for this change.

First, there has been a trend (encouraged by the European Commission) towards greater interest group activity at the Community level. At the planning stage, the Commission actively solicits the help of interested groups in drafting proposals for legislation. It asks the groups for factual and statistical information, and seeks their opinion on potential support for – or opposition to – its proposals. Anne Daltrop argues that this process has developed to the point where consultation has actually become an integral part of the legislative process.[8] Interested groups are given the opportunity to comment on draft legislation at almost every stage in the process. This may slow down the process of decision-making, but it also encourages active lobbying. The input of groups has even reached the point where some policy-makers have begun arguing that the more powerful interest groups are becoming too influential, and consultation needs greater regulation.

Secondly, membership of the Community has changed the constitutional context for groups. Before Britain joined the Community, British groups had only informal access to the domestic policy-making process, but very little formal or *de jure* access. Since Britain does not have the kind of constitutional court system that exists in countries like France, Germany and the United States, senior civil servants and ministers have usually been the last level of appeal. Philip Lowe notes that, before British entry,

> if you couldn't persuade senior civil servants or ministers, you really had no other right of appeal, because a majority government could always get its way. This had the effect of producing a rather tame environmental movement – it kept it pragmatic, reasonable, and responsible.[9]

Community membership has now given interest groups access to a weapon they have never had before: judicial review. By appealing through the European legal system to the European Court of Justice, they can serve a vital watchdog function by bringing more pressure to bear on the British government to implement EC environmental laws. In this sense, British groups now have similar opportunities to those enjoyed by American groups.

The third effect of Community membership on group tactics has been to give groups new outlets for lobbying, mainly in the form of the European Commission and the European Parliament. The Commission is the key point of access for the lobbyist, so interest groups try to win representation on Commission consultative committees and to establish long-term contacts with Commission departments.[10] Particularly since the institution of direct elections, the European Parliament has become increasingly important as a point of access, mainly because of its powers to amend or delay Commission proposals.

British groups have probably made more use of Community institutions than their counterparts in other EC countries. This is partly a result of their lack of satisfaction with the performance of the British government on environmental policy. David Baldock and Philip Lowe believe that because the British government has made few concessions on domestic environmental issues, British environmental groups have increasingly seen Brussels as a "court of redress" and a means of out-manoeuvring the government.[11] British groups also make more use of the Community because of their sheer numbers, and because they have a tradition of lobbying which groups in other EC countries do not. Britain has always had a strong role, for example, in the activities of the European Environmental Bureau. Philip Lowe points out that British groups are used to the "consultative, consensual style, and the endless discussions over draft legislation; that's the Whitehall style, British groups are used to it, and so they fit in very effectively at the European level".[12]

David Baldock suggests that groups in other countries are more ideological, more concerned with trying to "win hearts and minds" and less concerned with getting into the mechanics of individual projects. German environmental groups "prefer writing radical pamphlets, and not dirtying their hands dealing with official bureaucracies", says Baldock. "They don't tend to know what goes on in Brussels, and actually see the Commission as a threat to good environmental practice in (West) Germany."[13]

Philip Lowe sees a difference between "lead" and "lag" nations.

> Britain has been in the lead on the internal market debate because that fits in with domestic ideas of economic liberalism, but it has been lagging on environmental matters. In a "lag" state like Britain, the EC is seen as a progressive force. By contrast, the Germans, the Danes and the Dutch have been the lead states on environmental matters. In those countries, the Community actually puts a break on progress on environmental matters, so groups in those countries have a different outlook.[14]

German groups are further influenced by the existence of a relatively big and successful green party, which makes groups less important than in countries lacking an effective green party (although since their losses at the December 1990 all-German Bundestag elections, the future of the German greens has been in some doubt). Baldock also notes that environmental groups in France are weak, that those in Spain are at an early stage of development and that those in Italy are regionalized and diversified. Only Dutch and Danish groups take the same approach to Community institutions as British groups.

Although groups have been increasingly involved in recent years in lobbying the European Community, this is still a relatively new development. The result is that few groups have really begun to appreciate the potential of the Community as a policy-making body. This is mainly because their home constituencies are not constructed in a way that would make European law obviously relevant. Among those groups that *have* turned their attention to the Community, however, there has been an increasingly systematic approach to Euro-lobbying, and a clear trend towards seeing domestic environmental problems as part of Community-wide problems. In Britain, the Royal Society for the Protection of Birds (RSPB) offers a good example. The RSPB has been active in lobbying the Community, not simply for laws relevant to Britain, but for laws that would protect birds throughout the Community.[15] Lobbying at both the European and British levels began for the RSPB in the mid-1970s with the early stages of development of the 1979 directive on the conservation of wild birds. In 1979, the Society created an international office, operated part-time by Alistair Gammell.

Gammell believes that the Wildlife and Countryside Act was a primary factor in the RSPB decision to increase its use of European channels of lobbying. The Act, passed mainly in response to the EC birds directive (see Chapter 4), failed in the eyes of most environmentalists to give adequate protection to migratory birds, so the RSPB decided to increase its activity at the European level. Gammell's position became full-time in 1980. By March 1990, when the RSPB employed a new staff member to lobby the European Parliament, the number of full-time staff in the international office had grown to four.[16]

Another group that has become more active in the Community is the Institute for European Environmental Policy (IEEP), which works to "raise the level of debate about environmental policy-making in Europe".[17] IEEP began with an office in Bonn and a representative in London. An office was founded in Paris in 1978, and in London in 1980. The London office now has four full-time staff, and there are IEEP representatives in

Brussels and the Netherlands.

Meanwhile, some groups have begun opening new offices in Brussels. Until 1985, only the European Environmental Bureau (EEB) operated in Brussels. The Bureau was founded in 1974 (with the active encouragement of the European Commission)[18] as a conduit for the representation of environmental interest groups to the Community, particularly the European Commission. By 1982, the EEB represented sixty-three national environmental groups. It suffered consistently, however, from financial problems. Lowe and Goyder noted that while the EEB enjoyed considerable popular support in 1982, it was "a relatively new and weak interest in Brussels", that it relied "too heavily on the energies, qualities and interests of a tiny group of committed Euro-environmentalists", and that it did not "best use the resources potentially available to it in the knowledge, expertise, contacts and support of its overall membership".[19] Haigh notes the difficulties emerging from an internal debate about the functions of the EEB: whether it should serve the needs of its members or carry out independent lobbying.[20]

Partly because of the internal problems of the EEB, and partly because of the new realization of the importance of the Community as a policy-making institution, the second half of the 1980s saw new offices being opened in Brussels by Friends of the Earth, Greenpeace and the World Wide Fund for Nature – all interest groups with extensive international interests. (Other groups, such as the RSPB, have not opened full-time Brussels offices, but have employed full-time lobbyists.) David Baldock notes that while the opening of offices by other groups has tended to undermine the ability of the EEB to speak on behalf of Community environmental groups, the Bureau is still important as an umbrella group (although it continues to suffer a lack of money). Nigel Haigh feels that its value lies in its work as an umbrella body for those EC interest groups which mainly operate at the domestic level.[21] Generally, Baldock sees a long-term tendency towards the creation of more European networks of organizations, at both the voluntary and statutory levels.[22]

Pollution control and the European Community

In few other areas of environmental policy has the effect of Britain's membership of the European Community been more marked than in pollution control. The harmonization of environmental standards throughout the Community has meant not only the establishment of uniform air and water quality standards, but also the standardization of pollution control procedures. In contrast to the traditional British approach of voluntary compliance (see Chapter 5), other Community states believe in having clearly defined and mandatory air quality standards along American lines. The Thatcher administration was willing to accept only non-mandatory guidelines or reference levels, and put up strong resistance to EC Directives. This regularly put Britain out of line with other Community countries, on both air and water pollution. Britain may question the principles of EC policy, but it is ultimately obliged to accept that policy. Two issues in particular show how environmental policy has been influenced by the interplay between environmental groups, the British government and the Community: lead in fuel, and acid pollution.

Lead in petrol: domestic versus Community pressures

Road vehicles are a major source of the lead pollution implicated in damage to human health (it can lead to anaemia and neurological disorders, particularly in children). Lead was originally added to petrol to improve its performance in high compression engines. Removing the lead from petrol not only cuts airborne lead levels, but it is also essential for the operation of catalytic converters, fitted to vehicle exhaust systems to remove other pollutants from exhaust gases. In 1989, the British government introduced subsidies to promote the use of unleaded petrol. It was one of the last major industrialized countries to do this, and the decision only came after eighteen years of growing pressure on the government to remove lead from British petrol.

Lead in petrol first became a Community policy issue – and a British policy issue – in 1971. In that year, the Chief Medical

Officer to the British government recommended that airborne lead levels should not be allowed to increase above existing levels. The government concurred, and agreed to a staged reduction in the lead content of petrol from 0.84 grams per litre to 0.4g/l by 1976 (this was subsequently postponed until 1981 because of the oil crisis that followed the 1973 Arab–Israeli war). Also in 1971, the West German government agreed a faster staged reduction, to 0.15g/l by 1976. The European Commission set up two committees to study the health and technical effects of the problem, and a proposal for a Directive was issued in 1973 (the goals of which were also postponed by the 1973 oil crisis). At the time, Community countries had limits that varied from 0.84g/l to no limits at all. After much debate, the Community agreed its 1978 Directive, allowing member states to set limits at between 0.15 and 0.4g/l.

With the exception of the call made in 1973 by the Conservation Society for unleaded petrol, interest groups had almost nothing to say on the issue. This changed in 1977 with the creation of the Campaign Against Lead in Petrol (CALIP). By 1982, Britain had reduced its levels of lead from 0.84g/l to 0.4g/l, the maximum allowed under EC regulations. It planned a further reduction to 0.15g/l by 1985. Some environmentalists, however, felt that *all* lead should be removed, and lead in petrol became a broader public issue in 1982 with the creation of the Campaign for Lead-Free Air (CLEAR), directed by Des Wilson.

Since the late 1960s, Wilson had established a reputation as an aggressive campaigner on issues such as homelessness and freedom of information. His campaigning method involved a combination of direct lobbying and the tireless mobilization of public and media opinion. The CLEAR campaign began in January 1982 with a carefully managed public launch, backed by a story leaked to the *Observer*, and promoted by garnering the support of nearly 140 MPs and the leaders of the three main opposition parties.[23] This was followed by the judicious leak by CLEAR of a letter from Sir Henry Yellowlees, Chief Medical Officer of Health at the DHSS, to Whitehall colleagues warning of the dangers to children's health of lead in petrol. Within ten days of CLEAR's launch, the lead issue had been raised in the

House of Commons. Conservative MEP Stanley Johnson was then persuaded to table a motion in the European Parliament calling for lead-free petrol.

Early in the campaign, CLEAR had recognized the importance of amending the EC Directive to introduce lead-free petrol, so it made contact with European interest groups, and later helped co-ordinate the launch of a Community-wide campaign with the EEB and the European Bureau of Consumer Unions. The publication of American reports on the health risks of lead, together with CLEAR-sponsored studies in Britain, helped build momentum. On 18 April 1983, in its ninth report, the Royal Commission on Environmental Pollution (RCEP) recommended that the British government begin negotiations with the European Commission and other member states aimed at removing the minimum limit in the Directive, and effectively clearing the way for the earliest possible introduction of vehicles designed to run on unleaded petrol. Within thirty minutes of the publication of the RCEP report, the government had announced its agreement. It was still to be another six years before the government provided subsidies for lead-free petrol, but it nevertheless came.

Just how much impact CLEAR had on the British government's decision is contested. Professor Richard Southwood, chairman of the RCEP, claims the issue ultimately had little to do with CLEAR.[24] Des Wilson claims most (if not all) of the credit for CLEAR. In a period of fifteen months, he recalls, the CLEAR campaign was to achieve "a spectacular victory with a reversal of national policy and a decision in principle to move to lead-free petrol".[25] Wilson concedes the impact of the Royal Commission report on lead in petrol, and the contribution of the Conservation Society before the creation of CLEAR. However, asking whether the 1983 election may have been a factor in the government's decision, he argued that "lead-free petrol would have been irrelevant in the election if CLEAR had not politicized the issue to the point where it was a factor", and that "the Royal Commission only decided to look at the lead issue as a result of the CLEAR campaign".[26]

Derek Elsom makes a direct link between the mobilization

of public and media involvement achieved by CLEAR, the lobbying of British and Community politicians by CLEAR and the acceptance by the British government of the RCEP recommendation.[27] Nigel Haigh is less certain about the role of CLEAR. In 1984, he wrote that the public campaign "possibly" led to the government's acceptance of the RCEP recommendation,[28] while in 1986 he wrote that there was no doubt that "it was because of CLEAR that the Government responded ... so promptly and positively to the Royal Commission's recommendation for lead-free petrol".[29]

The motivation behind the British campaign on lead in petrol had been the *health* issue. Purely by coincidence, there was at the same time growing concern in West Germany about polluted forests. In order to cut vehicle pollution, it was proposed that catalytic converters be fitted to vehicles. Because these converters do not work with leaded petrol, there was mounting pressure in West Germany to introduce unleaded petrol in order to protect *forests*. The British government decision on unleaded petrol – involving the call for an amendment to the EC Directive – was taken in April 1983; in June, the West German government made a similar proposal.

"If it hadn't been for the West Germans coming into the issue," argues Haigh, "I don't think it would have been a foregone conclusion that the Directive would have been amended."[30] Elsewhere he observes that

> neither the [West] German government nor the British government can claim to have got lead out of petrol because neither could have done it alone. We have to recognize that we are locked into an international game. It follows that neither CLEAR nor the Royal Commission can make that claim either, though both can claim with some justice that without them it would not have happened.[31]

He also argues that if the EC had not existed, lead would have been taken out of petrol in Britain for domestic reasons (that is, through a combination of the CLEAR campaign and the RCEP recommendations). "The lead case isn't one where the

EC pushed Britain," he concludes, "but where Britain pushed the EC."[32]

The Community and acid pollution

If there is some question about the relative role of environmental groups and the EC in changing British policy on lead in petrol, there is much less question about their relative influences on the question of British acid pollution policy. In this case, British policy changed largely as a result of EC regulatory requirements – environmental groups were remarkably quiet on the issue.

In June 1988, the Thatcher administration approved the terms of the 1987 EC Directive on large combustion plants, thereby committing Britain to a 60 per cent reduction in sulphur dioxide (SO_2) emissions by the year 2003. (SO_2 is a primary component in the formation of acid pollution; Britain is the biggest emitter of SO_2 in Western Europe and the fourth biggest in the world.) The decision was notable because it came after several decades of opposition on the part of successive British governments to acid pollution control, and (especially since the late 1970s) of increasing criticism from many of Britain's European neighbours, notably Sweden and Norway, prime recipients of acid pollution generated outside their borders.

The first concerns about acid pollution were raised in the early 1970s by Scandinavian scientists and governments. A number of European countries, mainly those with smaller industrial bases and greater proportional imports of SO_2, began calling for a minimum of a 30 per cent reduction in SO_2 emissions from all countries. The larger industrial powers, for whom the costs of control would obviously be proportionally greater, were less enthusiastic. (France was one exception; it could afford to be an enthusiastic supporter of acid pollution controls since it generated most of its electricity from its rapidly expanding nuclear energy programme.) The most notable policy change came in 1982 when West Germany, in the wake of new evidence of growing acid pollution damage to its forests, and in the light of the growing popularity of the Green Party, abandoned its long-held opposition to controls. Concerned that its unilateral action would compromise the competitiveness of German industry by imposing the burden of the cost of pollution control, West Germany also began lobbying through the EC for Community-wide SO_2 reductions. The Commission immediately produced a series of proposals on pollution control, aimed at developing a comprehensive programme of Community legislation on air pollution.

Meanwhile, domestic pressure for change was also growing in Britain. Reports published during 1984 by the Royal Commission on Environmental Pollution, the environment committee of the House of Commons and the House of Lords European Communities committee subjected Mrs Thatcher's policies to closer scrutiny, and to criticism. The RCEP report described pollution control policy in Britain as suffering from inadequate resources, secretiveness, isolationism and a lack of forward planning and continuity.[33] The Commons and Lords reports argued that enough was known to justify the development and application of pollution control technology.[34]

British acid pollution policy was determined in large part by the then state-owned Central Electricity Generating Board (CEGB). From 1982, the chairman of the CEGB was Sir Walter Marshall (later Lord Marshall of Goring). Until privatization in 1990, the CEGB was Britain's largest electricity producer (accounting for 80 to 90 per cent of Britain's electricity), and produced about 60 per cent of the UK's total SO_2 emissions. Until the early 1980s, the CEGB was also the source of most of the scientific research on acidification in Britain. Throughout, the CEGB was unwilling to acknowledge any link between fossil fuels and acid pollution. It argued that cutting sulphur emissions would be of no proven benefit to the environment, and that the measures suggested in the 1984 Lords report would cost £2 billion, raise electricity costs by 10 per cent and increase unemployment. The CEGB also pointed with some satisfaction to the success of its postwar "tall stack" policy – equipping power-stations with tall smokestacks with the goal of dispersing the pollution to the winds. The tall stack policy indeed helped reduce London's once notorious smogs, but pollution dispersed to the winds does not magically disappear – it usually settles back on other people, other towns, other forests and sometimes other countries. In Britain's case, much of the pollution was settling on the Scandinavians.

Despite its hesitancy, the Thatcher administration did not always take criticism of its acid pollution policy lightly. In 1982, following the West German policy change, a review of acid rain policy was ordered within the Department of the Environment. DOE scientists concluded that reductions could best be achieved by fitting scrubbing equipment in several existing large power stations. In May 1984, Mrs Thatcher called a briefing session on government acid pollution policy, involving senior scientists and ministers. William Waldegrave and Martin Holdgate (then respectively environment minister and chief scientist at the DOE) argued that Britain should take a more positive position. They felt Britain should signal willingness to join the Thirty Per Cent Club (an informal association of countries committed to SO_2 reductions of at least 30 per cent) and take a positive line on NOx reduction. But objections from the Treasury, Lord Marshall and energy secretary Peter Walker persuaded Mrs Thatcher to defer any specific commitments.

Mrs Thatcher also faced criticism from members of her own party. The Bow Group, supported by ninety-five centre-left Conservative members of Parliament, argued in mid-1984 that the Conservative Party would "reap electoral credit" if the government was to agree to cut SO_2 and NOx emissions, and that Britain should join the Thirty Per Cent Club.[35] In December 1984, Conservative members of the European Parliament decided not only to join but to put themselves at the head of the majority group of MEPs critical of the British government position. Criticism of the CEGB meanwhile came from the Scandinavians, from the select committees of the Commons and the Lords, from government agencies such as the Nature Conservancy Council and from the Department of the Environment itself, which was privately very critical of the Board's attitude.[36] In September 1986, Lord Marshall finally admitted that the CEGB was at least partly to blame for Britain's acid emissions, and offered to spend £600 million by 1996 to cut those emissions (by controlling emissions from three coal-fired power-stations).

At first glance, the British record on acid pollution seems both unjustifiably stubborn and curiously contradictory. It was a British scientist, Robert Angus Smith, who first identified the problem in the 1850s. The 1863 Alkali Act was the first air pollution law in the world. One of the most common methods of controlling acid pollution – flue gas desulphurization (FGD), involving the attachment of scrubbers to smokestacks – was invented in Britain in the 1880s; Battersea power-station in London, opened in 1929, was the first power-station in the world to be fitted with FGD. The 1956 Clean Air Act, passed in response to the 1952 London smog, was the first comprehensive air pollution law of its kind, and the model for subsequent pollution laws elsewhere in the industrialized world.

Yet postwar British governments persistently refused to implement acid pollution controls. Britain's policy reversal in 1988 came after all industrialized nations save the United States had agreed to reduce emissions, and came thirty-four years after the Beaver Report of 1954 had concluded that the British Electricity Authority should reduce its SO_2 emissions, using scrubber technology. "We are not impressed by the speed with which these matters have been pursued," noted the authors of the report; while they agreed that scrubbers would be expensive and would add to electricity bills, "the cost of gas washing may well be justified by the advantages of a cleaner atmosphere and the human and material benefits that will follow".[37]

Britain had also refused to accede to domestic and international pressures despite mounting evidence of acid damage to British forests, lakes, rivers, wildife, crops and buildings. This evidence had generated mounting pressure on Mrs Thatcher from almost everyone: interest groups, scientists, other EC governments, senior Tory backbenchers, senior members of the Department of the Environment and Conservative members of the European Parliament. The Central Electricity Generating Board was almost alone in its support of government policy. All other EC countries had agreed to controls on acid pollution by 1985. The routine response of the Thatcher administration was to call for more research, and to argue that the expense of controlling acid pollution could not be justified until such time as there was scientific certainty about cause and effect. For most environmentalists, this was simply an excuse, and a cover for the real motives behind government policy: a general unwillingness to impose regulation on industry, and a specific unwillingness to place new financial burdens on the electricity generation industry at a time when the government was trying to reduce public spending and was also preparing the way for the privatization of the industry.

Ironically, with the 1988 decision to accede to the large combustion plant directive, the Thatcher administration not only agreed to reduce emissions, but went *well beyond* the goals of other European countries. It also went well beyond the demands of two previous agreements to which Britain had refused to accede: the 1979 Convention on Long-Range Transboundary Air Pollution (overseen by the UN Economic Commission for Europe, or ECE), and the Thirty Per Cent Club. Why had the Thatcher administration proved so stubborn on the acid pollution issue? There are several possible explanations.

First, as mentioned above, it seems likely that the government was concerned about imposing new costs and regulations on the electricity generation industry just as plans were being made for privatization.

Secondly, the government could afford to persist with its policy since criticism came mainly from quarters that were relatively easily contained. Government backbenchers had little influence; government ministers were easily replaced, shifted or overruled; and the protests of non-Community countries such as Sweden and Norway were less important than those of Community partners. The government was also more concerned with keeping the CEGB and British industry happy, and continuing its policy of reducing government regulation, than it was with keeping the environmental lobby happy. Besides, there was relatively little pressure from British environmental groups, most of which kept up their focus on countryside issues. Only groups such as Greenpeace, Friends of the Earth and the National Clean Air Society gave any appreciable attention to the acid pollution issue, at least until it became clear that forests and wildlife were being affected.

Thirdly, the traditional British policy position of voluntary restraints combined with three of the most important platforms of Thatcherism – free enterprise, reductions in public spending and deregulation – to work against the kinds of controls and increased investment demanded if acid pollution was to be successfully reduced.

Fourthly, acid damage was not as visible in Britain as it was in many other parts of Europe, partly because the damage took longer to make itself visible or evident, and partly because damage from acid pollution was not recognized as such. For example, most Londoners could see that the pollution which had made so many buildings in the city grimy and filthy was now under control, and the buildings themselves were being cleaned. London was less smoky, it was true, but levels of SO_2 and NOx (both of which are invisible) were still high.

Fifthly, part of the answer lies in understanding why pollution control in other countries *was* agreed. For France, with its rapidly expanding nuclear energy programme, the costs of acid pollution control were relatively small. In Germany, forests have considerable economic and cultural value; it was only when damage to the forests was clearly and widely *visible* – contributing in turn to the growing popularity of the Green Party – that the West German government agreed to action.

Sixthly, the structure of environmental policy-making in Britain meant that organizations like the CEGB had a considerable degree of freedom of action. As long as the CEGB (for whatever motives) remained unconvinced of the national economic benefits of reducing emissions, there was little likelihood of any substantive reductions in British emissions.

Finally, although Britain contributed to acid pollution damage elsewhere in Europe, it received relatively little pollution from outside its own borders; as little as 11 per cent of all acidity in British rainfall came from foreign sources.[38] Looking at the record on acid pollution in other countries, there was – in most cases – a direct relationship between the proportion of imported pollution, the environmental activism of the public and the policy response of the government. For example, a critical element in the policy calculations of Norway and Sweden was the fact that much of their pollution (45 to 65 per cent) was imported. Hence, (1) it would cost them relatively little to deal with their acid pollution problem; (2) even if they did deal with it, it would account for only a small proportion of the total pollution load; and (3) in order to deal with imported pollution, domestic action was needed to set an example. (Ironically, the country that stands to benefit most from a reduction in British emissions is Britain itself, which generates nearly 90 per cent of its own depositions.)

Against this background, why did Britain finally agree to control its sulphur dioxide and nitrogen oxides? Worsening relations with its old ally Norway certainly provided one key incentive. The growing weight of scientific evidence was another factor. West Germany did not agree to act until scientific evidence of forest death provided an irresistible motivation. Until 1987, Britain might have been able to believe that its forests were relatively unscathed by acid pollution damage, and the Thatcher administration may have been able to use scientific uncertainty as an excuse for not changing its policy. However, a report in 1987 by the UN Co-operative Programme for the Monitoring and Evaluation of Long-Range Transmission of Air Pollutants in Europe revealed that Britain had the highest percentage of damaged forests in Europe: 67 per cent of Britain's conifers were suffering slight to severe damage, and 28.9 per cent had moderate to severe damage.[39] Like the German government, the British government finally found itself moved by incontrovertible evidence.

The decisive event, however, was the adoption of the EC Directive on pollution from large combustion plants. Although the UN Economic Commission for Europe had been actively promoting attempts to reach international agreement on SO_2/NOx reductions, the European Community has made the greatest strides in actually implementing controls. In 1983, Gregory Wetstone and Armin Rosencranz described the Community as "the organization most likely to eventually succeed in establishing international SO_2 control programmes in response to Europe's transboundary pollution problem".[40] In 1988, it seemed that this had indeed become the case.

As with the leaded petrol issue, British policy on acid pollution was ultimately changed by a confluence of different influences. In this case, the EC was clearly the decisive influence where pressure from Scandinavia and the UNECE had had little effect. The environmental lobby helped prompt a response from the Community, but it was the Community that was ultimately responsible for the change in British policy.

Conclusions

Membership of the European Community has had a substantial effect on how environmental policy is made and implemented in Britain, on the tactics and activities of the British environmental lobby and on the approach of the Thatcher administration to environmental policy. Not only has membership led to a new debate about the existing environmental policy-making system in Britain, but it also obliged the Thatcher administration to take a more active role in designing policy. Where pressure from the domestic environmental lobby and other (non-EC) governments failed to influence British policy, Britain found itself being obliged to make concessions on EC policy in order to meet the requirements of EC law and to avoid becoming isolated within the Community. Community regulation not only compelled domestic policy changes on pollution and wildlife issues, but also substantially altered the outcome of the privatization of the water industry, and provided Britain with a stronger and more centralized water pollution control structure.

Membership of the Community also fundamentally altered the position and the powers of the environmental lobby. Groups can now often bypass domestic governmental institutions and appeal to a higher level of authority, and a more diverse array of institutions and legislative processes. Most notably, groups now have at their disposal the options of appeals to a policy-making system that is federal in all but name, and of the use of judicial review in forcing British government compliance with Community regulations.

8. The Changing Environmental Lobby

The 1980s saw far-reaching changes in the tactics and influence of the British environmental lobby, and in the place of the lobby in the public policy process. At the beginning of the decade, the lobby was already large and well supported. Through its contacts with ministers, peers, backbenchers and civil servants, and through its productive relations with the media, it had been able to help bring about significant policy changes, including amendments to many key pieces of legislation. To all intents and purposes, the lobby constituted the only significant opposition to government policy on the environment.

However, despite being arguably the largest social movement that Britain had ever seen, the lobby had less political influence than its numbers suggested. As an outsider interest, and a non-economic interest, it also had less influence than several other lobbies; for example, it did not have the same close working relationship with government as the farming lobby or the trade unions. The lobby also had a relatively limited view of environmental problems; much of the effort of most groups was directed at the single goal of protecting the countryside. Very few were interested in pollution issues, or international issues.

For its part, the British government in 1980 had very little understanding of the environment as a policy issue. The environment was low on the political agenda, Britain's environmental agencies were a confused, confusing and often ineffective rag-bag, and the body of environmental law was patchy at best. Britain lacked an environmental policy, a countryside policy and an energy policy. The result: Britain had many serious environmental problems, and there was little sign of any political will to address them.

By 1990, the position had changed. Politicians were taking more notice of the environment, public and political perceptions of the environment had changed, and the environmental lobby was bigger, wealthier, more professional, more active and more effective.

- Britain still lacked an environmental policy, but the debate about environmental policy had widened – more people and more policy-makers had a better understanding of the causes and effects of environmental problems.
- The membership of the environmental lobby had almost doubled, and its income had more than tripled.
- The environmental agenda had widened as new issues (domestic and global) emerged and old issues re-emerged. A combination of European Community activities and environmental lobby responses to electricity and water privatization had, for example, made air and water pollution more prominent public issues once again.
- Consumer issues became more prominent as more people were made aware of the role of individuals in causing environmental degradation. International issues (such as acid pollution) and global issues (such as global warming) became more prominent. As the influence of the farming lobby waned, so the influence of the environmental lobby on countryside issues increased.
- The lobby made ever more effective use of the media to promote public debate on environmental issues, and – through parliamentary committees and the European Community – had available substantial new channels for political influence.

There was also undoubtedly a growth in public awareness of environmental problems, in public concern for those problems and in public support for solutions to those problems. Opinion polls in the late 1980s repeatedly showed the environment as ranking high on the public issue agenda.

- A 1988 survey by the Department of the Environment found that 55 per cent of the population favoured environmental protection over growth.[1]
- A MORI poll in June 1989 found that nearly half the adult population (more than 18 million people) considered themselves environmentally conscious shoppers, and about 27 per cent said they were prepared to pay a 25 per cent price premium for a "green" product.[2]
- Perhaps the most revealing "poll" of all was the 2.25 million votes won by Green Party candidates at the European parliamentary elections in June 1989. By July 1989, the Green Party registered 7 per cent support in a MORI poll, as much as the SDP and the Democrats combined. By mid-1990, the party had 19,000 members.
- A MORI/*Times* poll in July 1989 found that more people (35 per cent) regarded green issues as vital than the National Health Service (29 per cent) and unemployment (24 per cent).

These changes were promoted by, and produced reactions from, an environmental lobby which saw fundamental changes in its structure, influence and effectiveness.

Changes in support for the environmental lobby

While the absolute number of environmental groups changed little during the decade, support for existing groups grew dramatically.

At the beginning of the decade, Lowe and Goyder put the membership of the British environmental lobby at between 2.5 and 3 million members. (It was probably closer to the lower figure, which meant that about 5 per cent of the population were members of environmental groups.) Based on the growth that took place in the bigger groups, but allowing at the same time for multiple membership (one person being a member of more than one group), the figure by the end of the decade was probably closer to 4.5 million (or 8 per cent of the population). (Lowe and Flynn put the figure at 3.5 to 4 million in 1989, while the *Economist* offered an estimate of 5 million members in early 1990.)[3]

One notable feature of this growth was that much of it was concentrated in the period from 1987 to 1989. In those three years, for example, membership of the Ramblers' Association doubled. In the eighteen months from July 1988 to December 1989, membership of Friends of the Earth grew by more than 200 per cent, from 39,000 to 120,000. Greenpeace membership had grown rapidly in the first half of the decade (by 500 per cent in the period 1980–85), but by 1989, Greenpeace had 320,000 members, 78 per cent of whom had joined since 1985. Even the Council for the Protection of Rural England, one of the smaller groups, saw a 25 per cent increase in its membership between 1988 and 1989.

Table 8.1: Changes in the membership of selected environmental groups (1980–89)

	1980	*1985*	*1989*	*% change 1980–89*
Greenpeace	10,000*	50,000	320,000	+3,100
FoE	12,000*	27,000	120,000	+ 900
WWF	51,000	91,000	202,000	+ 296
Ramblers	36,000	50,000	73,000	+ 103
National Trust	950,000	1,323,000	1,750,000	+ 84
CPRE	27,000	26,500	44,500	+ 65
RSNC	140,000	165,000	205,000	+ 46
RSPB	321,000	390,000	433,000	+ 35
Total	1,547,000	2,122,500	3,147,500	+ 103

Sources: *estimates; RSNC figures from the *Economist*, 3 March 1990; all other figures provided by groups; figures rounded out.

A second notable feature was the growth in support for the more activist environmental groups. In 1980, Greenpeace and Friends of the Earth were still less than a decade old, and were still small and relatively minor actors in the environmental lobby. Combined, they had less than half as many members as WWF, and less than 7 per cent of the membership of the RSPB. Despite continued growth in the sizes of WWF and the RSPB, Greenpeace – with a remarkable 3,100 per cent increase in membership – had 58 per cent more members than WWF by 1989. The combined membership of Greenpeace and FoE meanwhile *exceeded* that of the RSPB – see Table 8.1.

Impressive though growth in membership figures may be, it is not always seen by itself as a sign of strength. "Members are a good bargaining tool," argues Andy Wilson of CPRE, "but what wins the day is an intellectual case. Never mind the membership – is the *cause* popular? A small organization with a good case is more effective than a large organization with no case."[4] Growing membership is nevertheless indicative of a healthy lobby; not only does membership give people a direct, personal stake in the activities of interest groups, but growth in membership reflects growing support for the activities of environmental groups, and growing public commitment to the environmental cause.

Why did groups grow so rapidly during the decade, and especially in the period 1987–9? It is tempting to point to particular incidents, such as the Chernobyl disaster in April 1986, and Mrs Thatcher's autumn 1988 speeches. There were similar periods in earlier years when particular incidents caught the public imagination (such as the London smog of 1952, the publication of *Silent Spring* in 1962 and the *Torrey Canyon* disaster in 1967), and contributed to growth in support for groups. However, the sheer volume and scope of the changes in support for groups during the 1980s, the parallel growth in public interest in environmental issues and the response from government suggest that Chernobyl and the Thatcher speeches must be seen against a background of broader changes in social and economic attitudes.

Changes in support for environmental groups undoubtedly reflect growing public concern about environmental deterioration. The change may also be a result of the globalization of environmental issues that occurred during the decade. Neither global warming nor threats to the ozone layer were being addressed in any substantive form by the more traditional conservation groups. Among the larger environmental groups, only Greenpeace and Friends of the Earth focused much attention on these issues. Hence they would have been the groups to which new and younger environmentalists with more global concerns would have turned. Globalization may also help explain the growing support for the World Wide Fund for Nature, the only "traditional" British environmental group with a notably international focus. During the decade, WWF membership increased by nearly 300 per cent.

The growth in support for the environmental lobby may also be part of an undercurrent of radicalization occurring in the environmental movement. Certainly, more groups became more overtly politically active as the decade progressed. Frustration with the low priority given to the environment by the Thatcher administration, coupled with a growing sense of urgency about the need for action to curb environmental degradation, may have expressed itself in more uncompromising support for changes in policy on the part of younger and more impatient environmentalists. This may help explain why Greenpeace and Friends of the Earth saw such rapid growth. The issue of radicalization also helps explain why there is more overlap between the membership of the Green Party and that of Greenpeace and Friends of the Earth than there is between the Green Party and more traditional environmental groups.

To some extent, the growth of membership is also simply a result of more aggressive and effective recruitment drives by groups. For example, membership of CPRE, after remaining at about 26,000 to 27,000 through most of the early 1980s, increased to 36,000 in 1988 and to 44,500 in 1989. The key to this, argued CPRE, was "a more determined and professional effort to reach out to sympathetic members of the public and convert passive admiration for CPRE into active support".[5] A national membership structure was also created for the first time. A recruitment drive in Surrey in 1988 helped increase membership there from 250 to nearly 2,500 in six months, and

CPRE involvement in key public campaigns helped heighten its public standing at the local level; for example, CPRE involvement in the Channel Tunnel issue helped increase membership in Kent to 2,500.

With growing public support for the environmental lobby, growing policy interest in the issue and an extension in environmental group activity during the decade, there was also (not surprisingly) a sharp increase in the number of staff employed by environmental groups – see Table 8.2. Again, Greenpeace and Friends of the Earth saw the most impressive growth, from a combined staff of 20 in mid-decade to a combined staff of 160 by 1990.

Table 8.2: Increases in staff numbers at selected environmental groups

FoE	8 (1984)	80 (1989)	900% increase
BTCV	20 (1980)	150 (1989)	650% increase
Greenpeace	12 (1985)	80 (1990)	570% increase
WWF	50 (1980)	195 (1990)	290% increase
Ramblers	12 (1980)	28 (1989)	135% increase
National Trust	1,919 (1984)	2,383 (1988)	24% increase

Sources: information provided by groups.

Breaking down staff numbers by activity, there was a notable increase in staff responsible for lobbying and public information activities:

- In 1980, WWF had three staff working on policy issues; by 1990, it had a 32-member conservation department, in which at least nine staff worked on domestic policy-related issues. In 1980, WWF had two staff working in public relations; by 1990, the department had been expanded to include educational activities, and employed thirteen staff. A separate communications department employed another eight staff.
- The RSPB had by 1990 developed an international section responsible for European Community and international

affairs, a conservation planning section responsible for agriculture and forestry policy and a parliamentary affairs section with a staff member responsible for liaison with MPs and peers.

- In 1984, Friends of Earth had a total staff of eight; by 1989, it had nineteen staff working on campaigns alone, and a further eleven responsible for information.
- By 1990, CPRE had three staff working on policy issues, the Ramblers had three staff working in policy and campaigning, and Greenpeace had one full-time lobbyist, together with support staff.

Parallel with the growth in membership and staff, there was growth in the income of environmental groups – see Table 8.3.

Table 8.3: Changes in the income of selected environmental groups (£000s)

	1980	*1985*	*1989*	*% change 1980–89*
Greenpeace	175*	600	4,500	+2,470
BTCV	500	n.a.	9,000	+1,700
WWF	1,646	4,601	20,760	+1,160
FoE	200*	414	2,902	+1,350
Ramblers	147	n.a.	1,193	+ 710
CPRE	145	n.a.	755	+ 420
RSPB	2,724	6,976	13,268	+ 390
National Trust	24,560	37,328	55,800	+ 127
Total	30,097	n.a.	108,178	+ 260

Sources: information provided by groups; *estimates.

The National Trust held its position as the wealthiest of the groups. (To be accurate, much of the money it raises goes to protecting Britain's cultural heritage, and so cannot really be counted as money spent on environmental protection.) The Trust increased its fund-raising staff from three to seventeen between 1985 and 1989.[6] While it more than doubled its already substantial income during the decade, several other groups saw a relatively spectacular growth in income. For example, the income of WWF increased by nearly 1,200 per cent between 1980 and 1989, making the Fund by far the wealthiest British interest group dealing solely with environmental issues. Greenpeace saw an even more spectacular rise in income, from about £175,000 in 1980 to about £4.5 million in 1989, an increase of almost 2,500 per cent. The total income of the environmental lobby in 1989 was in the region of £170 million, a 350 per cent increase over 1980.

Changes in the tactics of environmental groups

At the same time as the growth in the size of – and support for – environmental groups, there were also a number of changes in the tactics and methods of those groups during the decade.

While many of the more "traditional" groups were concerned about their charitable status in the early 1980s, and hesitant about directly criticizing government or overtly lobbying Parliament, ministers and civil servants, there was a tendency towards closer monitoring of government activities. This often resulted in overt criticism of government policy and overt attempts to make policy suggestions public. Alan Mattingly of the Ramblers' Association believes that, thanks to better co-ordination, greater professionalism and improved resources, groups are now generally "more forthright in presenting their views than hitherto. It has also derived, in part, from our confidence that we speak for a very wide cross-section of public opinion."[7]

While the traditional groups have tended to become more politically influential, the more activist groups of the early 1980s have, if anything, become more conservative, and more centrally a part of the "establishment" environmental lobby. In 1980, for example, Greenpeace was very much on the periphery of the lobby. While it had good contacts with other groups, its methods were unique: a reliance on confrontation and the staging of events geared towards catching media headlines. This tended to distance Greenpeace from the more traditional groups. It was also relatively small, with a staff of a dozen, a membership of 10,000 and an income of about £175,000. Since then, it has not only seen a remarkable growth in its size, support and wealth, but it has also become less confrontational, and more inclined to use the same tactics of lobbying and discreet political influence once reserved by the more conservative groups. Much the same has happened to Friends of the Earth.

Parallel with the growth in political activism, there was a tendency during the decade for groups to move away from complaint and criticism, and towards research-based appeals to policy-makers, industry and the public, and towards the provision of services and solutions. In 1980, many groups and their supporters tended to see environmental problems as being caused by the uncaring values of industry and government, and to focus on the consequences of environmental degradation, particularly the loss of wildlife, countryside and habitat. By 1990, there was a new emphasis on the role of the individual in the creation of environmental problems, and on proposing solutions to the problems, rather than simply warning of their consequences.

Nigel Haigh noted in 1990 that "Groups used to have a table-thumping role. Now there is no need for that. What we need is people who can tell us what needs to be *done*."[8] This has happened most notably at Friends of the Earth, once well known for its confrontational campaigning, demonstrations and events aimed at catching media attention. Its partly confrontational anti-CFC campaign was replaced by advice-based campaigning when it commissioned a technical report aimed at giving the construction industry specific advice and information on CFC use (see Chapter 6). FoE also co-operated with CPRE and WWF in commissioning a report from Sussex University on the environmental implications of electricity privatization.[9]

There was little change during the decade in the way of formal co-ordination between groups, but *ad hoc* co-ordination was maintained and has grown. There was a notable growth in the publication of joint statements on government policy. Some examples:

- a co-ordinated response in 1988 by nine of the largest conservation and amenity groups to the government's set-aside policy, in which farmers are paid to leave their land out of production;
- the pamphlet *Greening the Bill*, published in response to electricity privatization by CPRE, WWF, FoE and the Association for the Conservation of Energy;
- the publication of authoritative research on the environmental effects of electricity privatization (CPRE/FoE) and water privatization (CPRE/RSPB/WWF);
- *Blueprint for a Green Europe*, a checklist of policy suggestions prepared in anticipation of the 1989 European elections by FoE, CPRE, WWF and the Green Alliance;
- *The Green Gauntlet*, a checklist of practical environmental measures proposed to the government in a pamphlet published jointly by WWF, Greenpeace and FoE.

Groups generally believe that co-ordination is good, with groups working well together on an *ad hoc* basis as and when issues of common interest arise. Jonathon Porritt suggests that while the co-ordination of group activities may sometimes seem incoherent and unco-ordinated, most groups are working towards more or less pre-agreed sets of goals. The role of groups is often complementary. Porritt notes how Friends of the Earth, in working with other groups on changes to the water privatization bill, was often cast as the confrontational group. By taking on this role, it attracted enough of the ire of ministers involved to allow other groups to portray themselves as less confrontational, and to succeed in having some of their proposals accepted.[10] He admits, however, that greater co-ordination is needed. During 1989, Friends of the Earth discussed the problem internally, mainly because it felt the environmental movement needed a co-ordinated strategy for the next general election; suggestions were being made for a strategy conference involving all major groups.

There were also several changes during the decade relating to the access of environmental groups to the policy-making process. First, in the area of countryside conservation, the decline of the farming lobby, the reduced power and influence of the National Farmers' Union and growing criticism of MAFF combined to reduce the influence of the agricultural lobby, while allowing environmental groups more influence. The British government still lacks a countryside policy, and many of the changes in the countryside against which groups campaigned so actively in the early 1980s continue unabated. Nevertheless, there was a discernible shift in public opinion and sympathy away from the agricultural lobby and towards the conservation lobby.

Secondly, the new system of parliamentary committees introduced in 1979 led to an increase in the opportunities afforded to groups to influence Parliament. The House of Commons environment committee has been of obvious value, but groups also found a sympathetic ear in the science and technology committee and the European Communities committee of the House of Lords. Parties too became more responsive. Porritt notes that one of the effects of Mrs Thatcher's 1988 speeches on the environment was to promote increased demand for better environmental policies in the Conservative Party.[11] This led, among other things, to the creation of the Tory Green Initiative, aimed both at making government ministers more aware of green issues and at communicating government policies to the public. Because Conservative backbenchers became more interested in environmental issues, Friends of the Earth in 1989 spent more of its time and resources on direct ministerial and backbench lobbying, and had plans to appoint a parliamentary liaison officer for the first time.[12]

Finally, and most importantly, with the realization that an increasing amount of British environmental policy and law is now influenced by or decided in Brussels, there was a tendency during the second half of the decade for groups either to increase their direct representation at the Community level, or to pay more attention to EC legislation and its implications for Britain. In its 1988 annual report, CPRE noted "the increasing influence wielded" by the EC over domestic affairs. "While this has long been the case on much agricultural and environmental policy, the approach of 1992 means that Europe's influence will intensify on all of CPRE's main concerns."[13] Friends of the Earth reduced its lobbying of the British government and backbenchers in 1987–8, and decided to concentrate instead on European bodies.[14] It had plans in 1989 to appoint a Community lobbyist in Brussels, following the examples of Greenpeace and the World Wide Fund for Nature.

Another clear change in tactics during the 1980s involved environmental groups paying more attention to public attitudes and behaviour. The growth of the green consumer movement was at least in part an outcome of the public awareness activities of the environmental lobby during the decade. As green consumerism grew, groups found a new and potentially fruitful means of influencing public policy through encouraging changes in consumer demands. Not only were groups now exerting pressure on the British government through the European Community, but – by building an environmentally educated consumer population – they could exert further pressure for policy change.

More generally, the environmental lobby continued to exert pressure for policy changes by building on its good contacts with the media. Thanks partly to media activities by environmental groups in the 1970s and early 1980s, partly to Mrs Thatcher's statements on environmental issues from 1988 and partly to the globalization of the environment, the media in Britain (as elsewhere in the West) responded by giving new prominence to environmental issues. Most larger groups have full-time press and public relations departments, most of which grew in size during the Thatcher years.

By 1989, it was difficult to open a national newspaper without seeing some coverage of environmental or green consumer issues. Media enthusiasm for the environment reached the point where use of the word "green" almost became hackneyed and trite. Early in the decade, few national papers had their own environment or planning correspondents; between 1988 and 1989 alone, the number of national newspapers with environmental correspondents grew from five to twelve.[15] The *Observer*, most of whose environmental stories during the early 1980s had emanated from Geoffrey Lean, its sole environmental correspondent, had an environment staff of six by 1990. By 1989–90, every group had reported a growth in the number of staff working on media activities, and in requests for information. Greenpeace in 1990 had a press office of four staff, and a public information department responding to 140,000 written requests for information each year.[16]

New groups were formed during the decade specifically to take advantage of – and promote – media interest in the environment. The Television Trust for the Environment (TVE) was founded in 1984 to co-produce, promote, finance and distribute TV and video programmes on the environment. In 1988, Media Natura was founded to build a data base of media companies and professionals willing to work on environmental awareness issues at reduced rates. Media Natura acts as a go-between, noting the specifications for a project required by a conservation group, finding appropriate media sponsors and overseeing the completion of the project. In its first year, Media Natura had managed forty projects for more than two dozen groups. The projects had a market value of £370,000, but were completed at a saving of almost 80 per cent.[17]

Another change during the decade was the more positive relationship that developed between groups and the statutory conservation agencies. At the beginning of the decade, it was common to find groups criticizing the agencies. The 1984 views of Pye-Smith and Rose are illustrative: they argued that the "authority, confidence and capability" of the NCC had gone into sharp decline since 1973, that its ruling council was "obsessively secretive" and that the Council had "failed to speak out effectively or to make full use of its legal powers".[18]

By the end of the decade, there were signs of greater co-operation and understanding between groups and agencies. In 1989, when the government announced plans to break up the NCC and the Countryside Commission, environmental groups were quick to come to the defence of the agencies, and were unanimous in their condemnation of government proposals. Noting, for example, that the NCC had helped end tax incentives for tree planting on ecologically important bogland sites in Scotland, the countryside campaigner for Friends of the Earth voiced his suspicion that the NCC was "being punished for having stood up to the government on these and other issues".[19] The RSNC wrote to the environment secretary, saying the proposals were "nothing short of a disaster".

Groups generally became more professional during the decade, particularly in their approaches to raising money, raising public awareness and exerting pressure on the policy process. Changes at WWF were particularly notable. In 1980, the Fund was housed in relatively cramped offices in central London, and still exhibited many of the signs of a charity concerned with saving appealing animals. In 1981, amid some controversy, a decision was taken to move the Fund out of London, to recruit new and more professional senior managers and to take a more professional attitude towards fund-raising. It was also decided to focus less on threats to wildlife (a *symptom* of environmental destruction more generally) and more on addressing the broader problem of environmentally destructive development. In 1986, WWF director George Medley noted that the Fund wanted "to get away from the cuddly image of an organization concerned only with fluffy animals in tropical countries and show that we have the needs of the wider natural environment very much at the heart of our objectives".[20] Hence the Fund's decision in 1988 to change its name from "World Wildlife Fund" to "World Wide Fund for Nature" (an attempt to indicate its broader interests while keeping the same initials).

Medley also argues that WWF is now a much more professional organization, using modern business and marketing methods, while remaining conscious of its charitable status. The same could be said of the many other environmental groups that saw substantially increased income during the decade. WWF's primary goal in the 1980s was to create a triangular relationship between environmentalists, policy-makers and business. Medley points not only to persuasion by WWF to convince the Overseas Development Administration to carry out environmental impact analyses of its projects, but also to campaigning by WWF to encourage industry to manufacture products less damaging to the environment.[21].

The changing place of the environmental lobby

Despite the undoubted growth in the size and influence of the environmental lobby, and despite greater public awareness of the nature of environmental issues, two fundamental questions remain.

First, was the environmental lobby able to capitalize on its growing power during the decade? In the early 1980s, Lowe and Goyder felt it had not capitalized on its existing power and influence. By the end of the decade, opinions on this were divided. Alan Mattingly, director of the Ramblers' Association, noted in 1990 that the Association was being consulted more frequently by government departments on issues of concern to the organization. He felt that there was no doubt that the Ramblers were more influential in 1990 than they had been in 1980.

> I think central government is certainly taking environmental groups more seriously than they were ten years ago. This is probably mainly due to the growth in membership of environmental organizations and the evident growth in public concern about environmental issues. However, it is one thing for the government to listen and talk to environmental groups more frequently; it is quite another for them to frame their policies along lines advocated by us.[22]

Jonathon Porritt believes that the lobby became more successful during the decade than the public – or the lobby itself – knew, and that it was simply bad at publicizing its successes.

"Ten years ago, the influence of environmental groups on the government was negligible," he argues.

> It's true to say that, in terms of formal policy changes, the cupboard is still pretty bare today. But in terms of creating a new level of awareness among Tory supporters and voters, the environmental movement has done a fantastic job. It held the line on many issues, and had breakthroughs on others, like the ozone layer, vehicle emissions, waste management and the National Rivers Authority. But the movement hasn't done a good job of explaining how much it has achieved. Groups are still not used to being successful. There's a psychological problem with success.[23]

The environmental lobby was undoubtedly the major influence on public opinion on the environment, and through the public arena has exerted considerable influence on the government. It also learned to work through the European Community more effectively. Using this combination of public pressure and Community pressure, it was able to bring about some substantial changes in public policy during the decade. At the same time, much British environmental policy was also determined by Community legislation, and by the often unforeseen consequences of Thatcherism itself, rather than by the efforts of the lobby alone.

The second question relates to whether or not the environmental lobby has a sense of direction. Again, opinion on this is divided. Bill Adams believes that the conservation lobby lost direction in the second half of the decade. The response to proposed changes in the state conservation agencies brought some focus, he argues, but essentially there was little to focus the attention of conservation groups after the Wildlife and Countryside Act was passed. He believes this is partly because the countryside was by 1990 less prominent as an issue, and also because the Thatcher administration was providing fewer challenges to groups and more solutions to environmental problems.[24]

On the other hand, groups have always been clear about the issues that need to be addressed, they have learned much more about how to use the political system to bring pressure to bear for policy changes; and they have generally become more professional and more powerful. The course of environmental policy took a number of unexpected changes in direction during the decade (for example, the growing significance of the green consumer, the prominence of pollution issues during the 1980s and the globalization of environmental issues), and groups responded well to these changes. Their goals in 1990 – as in 1980 – were to continue direct, practical environmental management and protection, and to continue exerting pressure for change in public and political attitudes to the environment.

As a result of the growth in public interest in the environment during the 1980s, it became patently obvious that British environmental law and the network of environmental agencies in Britain were woefully inadequate. It became increasingly clear that the structure was ill designed to cope with an issue that cut across the responsibilities of most existing government departments. The weaknesses in the Department of the Environment, and the inaptness of its very title, became particularly evident. Only with the appointment of Chris Patten as environment secretary in 1989 was the department administered – for the first time – by someone willing to give the environment more prominence in the affairs of the department than its other responsibilities in housing and local government.

It also became more obvious during the decade that the division of other environmental responsibilities among government departments dealing with energy, transport and agriculture was inefficient. The response of Mr Patten to some of these problems was to propose the creation of a cabinet committee to draw up a government white paper on the environment. Not only did Mrs Thatcher agree to chair the committee, but the inclusion on the committee of all ministers whose departments have environmental responsibilities had the effect of concentrating minds on the parameters of the issue. The white paper was duly considered during the course of 1990, While it seemed to confirm the new place of the environment on the British policy agenda, and a new desire by government to assess environmental issues rationally, the final white paper – published in September 1990 – indicated that hopes for a new prominence for environmental policy were to be postponed again.

9. Environmental Politics in Britain

At the beginning of the 1980s, the nature of environmental politics in Britain was exposed as never before by the debate over the Wildlife and Countryside Act of 1981. The way the original bill was debated, the role of the environmental lobby in that debate and the principles that determined the final form of the bill when it was passed into law – all these combined to reveal a government that understood little about environmental policy, and an environmental lobby that was large and well organized, but not powerful.

In the years that followed, the nature of the environmental debate changed. For many different reasons – the influence of the environmental lobby, the influence of the European Community, rising public awareness, the emergence of a newly concerned consumer, the relative decline of the agricultural lobby and the politicization and globalization of the environment – the debate had broadened by 1990. If the Wildlife and Countryside Act was the event that ushered in the decade, then the 1990 white paper on the environment was the event that closed the decade. The two events offer useful points of reference and comparison.

The 1990 white paper

At the autumn 1989 Conservative Party conference, environment secretary Chris Patten announced that the government was to begin work on a white paper on the environment. A white paper by definition is a statement on resolved government policy. White papers are normally preceded by green papers, which are discussion documents intended to elicit opinions and debate prior to the agreement of a white paper. In the case of the environment, this preparatory stage was eliminated. Mrs Thatcher herself chaired the cabinet committee that oversaw the preparation of the paper, and the government heralded its publication by describing it as something of a Beveridge Report on the environment, a fundamental and permanent shift in the direction of policy.

On 25 September 1990, the government published the white paper under the title *This Common Inheritance*. The paper listed more than 350 measures already being taken by the government on various environmental issues, along with a few proposals for new legislation or new activities. Among the few new initiatives:

- The creation of a ministerial energy efficiency committee under the energy secretary, aimed at countering global warming by limiting CO_2 emissions from power stations and road vehicles.
- New proposals to protect the countryside, including more protection for hedgerows and controls on some new farm buildings.
- Changes in the institutional arrangements for environmental policy-making, including the continuance of the cabinet committee on the environment set up to oversee production of the white paper, and the naming of ministers with environmental responsibilities in each government department.
- A programme to combat noise nuisance.
- Reflecting once again the insistence by British policy-makers on including the built environment under the general heading of "the environment", proposals to further protect Britain's architectural heritage, including cathedrals.

Among the media, opposition parties and environmental

groups, the white paper was almost universally condemned as disappointing and as a missed opportunity. Opposition from interest groups was perhaps predictable, given the continuing differences of opinion between the government and the environmental lobby; what was less predictable was the *depth* of opposition from the lobby. Much had been made by the Thatcher administration in the autumn of 1989 about plans for the white paper. As the writing of the paper progressed, groups expressed growing doubts about its goals and content. Upon its publication, several groups said it was even worse than they had expected. Peter Melchett, executive director of Greenpeace, said: "Nobody realized it would be this bad. The government has dodged the important issues by reiterating existing inadequate policies and has avoided making any new commitments."[1]

For media and groups alike, it seemed that Chris Patten had been outvoted not only by the Prime Minister but also by his cabinet colleagues. In a leader, *The Times* noted that Mr Patten had fought "a titanic struggle" within Whitehall for a more ambitious approach to environmental pollution, but had been opposed by cabinet colleagues, notably Cecil Parkinson (transport), John Wakeham (energy) and John Major and Norman Lamont (Treasury).

"These other politicians are not personally anti-green, nor is Mrs Thatcher," argued *The Times*.

> They oppose green policies because, in the corridors of Whitehall, they are not free agents but regard themselves as delegates of interest groups: the oil and gas companies, the motoring lobby, road builders, and that sternest of all short-termers, the Treasury as guardian of the retail price index, and thus of the government's electoral fortunes.

The Times went on to argue that the white paper, which had been born partly of "political panic" following the 15 per cent showing of the Greens in the 1989 European elections, had lost political impetus through a combination of the decline of the green vote and "the old ways of Whitehall".[2]

Several of the proposals that had been made by Patten, most

of them built on market-based policies to reduce pollution, were excluded from the paper. One notable exclusion was a graduated "carbon tax" proposed by Patten to make the use of CO_2-producing fossil fuels more expensive. Michael McCarthy, environment correspondent for *The Times*, reported that this had been abandoned because of the opposition of energy secretary John Wakeham, who was opposed to any proposals that might increase the cost of electricity prior to the privatization of the electricity supply industry. It had also been opposed by Mrs Thatcher and by John Major (then Chancellor of the Exchequer) because of its potential effect on inflation. A goal of stabilizing CO_2 emissions by the year 2000 had to be postponed to the year 2005, mainly due to the opposition of transport secretary Cecil Parkinson, who preferred no target at all.[3]

The white paper was undoubtedly tentative and hesitant, and far from revolutionary. While government critics could take issue with many of the details of the paper, the values and principles underlying it are more important. Against the background of Thatcherism generally, specific policies of the Thatcher administration and the values and policies of British governments as a whole, the paper reveals several points of significance.

First, despite everything she had done and said after the autumn of 1988, Mrs Thatcher's interest in the environment in 1990 was still clearly conditional and tentative. When seen against her autumn 1988 statements, the paper looks particularly weak and unimaginative. Her 1988 statements seemed bold, but when it came to working up detailed policies, she still clearly placed short-term concerns about inflation, government spending, business regulation and privatization above long-term protection of the environment.

Secondly, the British government still has a limited and unimaginative definition of environmental policy. Michael McCarthy noted the day after publication of the white paper that, although some of the brightest minds in the DOE had been brought to bear on the paper, the principal civil servants involved "had an intimate knowledge of housing and local government policy but, at the beginning of the exercise, much less knowledge or experience of environmental questions". Their involvement, he argued, illustrated "the lowly status long accorded the issue of environmental protection in the government department normally entrusted with its care".[4]

Finally, economic interest groups still have considerable influence within Whitehall. Notable among these are the transport, oil and gas, and business lobbies. Despite its growing public support, the environmental lobby still has not been able to convert public sympathy into substantial political influence.

Environmental politics in Britain

This book set out to assess the place and the influence of the environmental lobby in the British policy process, and specifically to ask how the lobby responded to changes in the outlook, priorities and philosophies of governing of the Thatcher administration, a government very different from its predecessors. It has tried to identify changes in the strategies and tactics of groups, to measure the extent to which those strategies and tactics have succeeded, and to use the example of the environmental lobby to assess the extent to which Thatcherism under Mrs Thatcher has proved to be a collectivist or confrontational style of governance. To close, five specific questions will be posed and addressed.

(1) Thatcherism: is it different?

There is much debate about the extent to which Thatcherism represents a departure from the policies and values of preceding administrations. Answering this question is complicated by the fact that so many Thatcherite policies evolved over time, rather than being set out in a comprehensive platform in 1979. Some even doubt whether there is such a thing as "Thatcherism". Paul Hirst, for example, writes of the "mirage of Thatcherism", and argues that it is a myth propagated by the right, the left and the media, each for their own purposes.[5]

However, to seek consistent, distinct policies is not only to miss the essence of Thatcherism, but also perhaps to miss the essence of political leadership. Politics is often instinctive rather than premeditated, and Thatcherism has been no exception. Peter Riddell puts it well: "Thatcherism is a personal, highly distinctive, approach to politics rather than a coherent set of ideas. Mrs Thatcher is not a great political thinker or theorist."[6] Elsewhere, he argues that "Thatcherism is essentially an instinct, a set of moral values and an approach to leadership rather than an ideology."[7]

This book is based on the premise that there is a body of values, a series of policies and a particular style of governance that add up to Thatcherism and that much of this will survive though Mrs Thatcher has left office. While not all of Mrs Thatcher's policies were original, while many of her actions were reactive rather than pre-emptive and while she was not always consistent, the character and substance of her administration were significantly different from those of her predecessors. Mrs Thatcher, for example, used the powers inherent in the office of prime minister to a greater extent than most of her predecessors. The personality of the prime minister is not often a factor in how British government is managed, yet Mrs Thatcher stamped a distinctive style on the office. Her devotion to duty, her grasp of detail, her enthusiasm, her belief in the rightness and the morality of her values and policies and her insistence on the loyalty and collective responsibility of the cabinet marked her style as significantly different from those of her predecessors.

As regards her policies, Mrs Thatcher wrought some substantial and often obvious changes on Britain; Britain today is a very different place from the Britain of 1979.

- Income tax is lower, the middle class is bigger and wealthier, and there are signs of a new entrepreneurial spirit in Britain. There was an average net increase of 500 new firms every week from 1979 to 1989, and the number of self-employed people rose during the 1980s by more than a third.[8]
- Trade unions are weaker, and their leaders are significantly less prominent in public life.
- There were three times as many individual shareholders

in 1989 as in 1979,[9] and three million more private home owners (making home ownership figures in Britain among the highest in the industrialized world).[10]

- The public sector has shrunk by a factor of two-thirds, and privatization has been consciously copied overseas.
- Many institutions (notably local government, universities and the health services) have been obliged to become more self-reliant and self-supporting.
- At least partly in response to Thatcherism, the policies of opposition parties have often changed, occasionally quite dramatically, as in the abandonment by Labour of its unilateralist policies.

In other areas, life in Britain has either changed little, has changed for the worse or has changed in ways that were perhaps not anticipated by Mrs Thatcher. Regional divisions and the divide between rich and poor have grown, the position of women and ethnic minorities has improved little, crime rates rose sharply during the decade (by more than 5 per cent annually between 1980 and 1987), Britain is still a notoriously reluctant European, and spending on public services and social security has actually risen (by two-fifths in real terms in the case of the latter).

As for environmental policy, Mrs Thatcher undoubtedly surprised environmentalists in 1988–9 with her apparently newfound interest in global warming and threats to the ozone layer. Despite claiming that there would be no U-turns and no alternative courses of action, she often changed direction dramatically, notably on the issues of acid pollution, water pollution control and nuclear power. In 1979, she had no environmental policy to speak of, and in her first two administrations, she proved largely unresponsive to the demands of the environmental lobby. By 1989–90, whether through her own volition, through the power and influence of the environmental lobby or through circumstances beyond her control, she was paying significantly greater attention to environmental problems. In this alone, she was markedly different from her predecessors. True, many of her policies amounted either to political opportunism or to responses to unanticipated circumstances, and the extent to which she was responding to environmental problems in any meaningful policy sense was debatable. Generally, however, there is little question that the environment achieved a new prominence on the public policy agenda in Britain during the Thatcher years, and most notably after Mrs Thatcher's speeches in the autumn of 1988.

(2) Has there been a lasting Thatcher revolution?

Simply put, it is too early to say. Now that Mrs Thatcher is no longer Prime Minister, only time will reveal the level of endurance of her values and policies. It is difficult to think of many of her key policies being undone. Private home ownership is unlikely to decrease; the size of the middle class is unlikely to fall, many new shareholders may well retain their taste for investment, it is unlikely that future non-Conservative governments would consider substantial renationalization of privatized industries, and the enterprise culture is likely to persist, if not because of Thatcherism then certainly because of the new demands made of British industry with the creation of the single European market. Similarly, it is unlikely that the new prominence of environmental issues during the 1980s will decline substantially in the short term, and it is difficult to see the environment losing its newly prominent position in the policy platforms and manifestos of all the larger British political parties.

Mrs Thatcher responded to a widely recognized problem: the failure of Britain to adjust effectively to the new circumstances of the postwar world. Until the mid-1970s, it seemed that many Britons were unable or unwilling to recognize, acknowledge or understand the reasons for Britain's relative economic and political decline, unable to understand the economic implications of the end of Empire, and unable to recognize that Britain had to learn to compete in a new global economic system. Further, they seemed unwilling to learn to become European, to accept Britain's commitments to the European Community and to recognize the benefits of EC membership. While Mrs Thatcher was never an enthusiastic European, she responded to the arguments of those who felt British industry should become more efficient and competitive, and that Britons should become more competitive and entrepreneurial.

While many of the goals of Thatcherism will probably have an enduring appeal to many voters, Mrs Thatcher's *methods* are less likely to remain a lasting feature of British politics, not that they were ever really intended to be. Mrs Thatcher believed that the British disease needed urgent and probably unpalatable treatment, and that life for Britons would worsen before it improved. While many of the changes she wrought in the 1980s may endure, the methods needed to pursue those changes will become less relevant. A new post-Thatcherite generation of Conservative leaders had already begun emerging in the late 1980s, people who were influenced and tempered by Thatcherite economics and conviction politics, but whose methods are different. Now that John Major – one of the leaders of that generation – is in 10 Downing Street, it remains to be seen how different the new generation will be from its predecessors.

(3) Has the relationship between groups and government changed?

Before 1979, there were signs of a consensus in some areas of British politics. There was frequent consultation, for example, between the government and trade unions, the agricultural lobby and the business lobby. In other words, there was much consultation on economic interests, and much of the policy process was determined and influenced by such consultation.

It now seems clear that when Mrs Thatcher spoke in the late 1970s and early 1980s of the dangers of consensus, she was really thinking about "creeping socialism" (including the high cost of welfare and Britain's large public sector), and referring to the power and influence of trade unions. Because of her dislike for socialism, welfare and state planning, she was clearly resentful of the influence exerted by unions on government. When she spoke of the end of consensus, she did not mean that the government would stop consulting with all interests. Rather, she meant the end of access for groups that she disagreed with, notably trade unions.

There is no doubt that the relationship between trade unions and the government has changed dramatically, and that the unions and their leaders no longer have anything like the power and influence they had in the early 1980s. The agricultural lobby, meanwhile, has declined for reasons other than deliberate government policy. The assault of the environmental lobby has combined with growing public resentment at the wealth of farmers and disquiet about the quality of British agricultural produce to reduce the influence of the agricultural lobby.

However, the business lobby retains much influence within government. While Mrs Thatcher was not as hostile to the environmental lobby as she was to trade unions, neither was she particularly open to its overtures. During her third administration, she apparently recognized the importance of some aspects of environmental policy, but not to such an extent as to encourage substantial consultation with environmental groups. The environmental lobby improved its contacts with government and its influence with the public during the 1980s, but there was still one fundamental difference between environmentalism and Thatcherism that counted against much real agreement between them: while the lobby was generally in favour of regulation and government intervention to treat environmental problems, Mrs Thatcher preferred to leave environmental planning to the free market.

Only in the late 1980s did the environmental lobby really begin seriously to consider the power of the consumer in approaching environmental problems, and the possibilities of arguing the economic benefits of environmental management.

(4) Consensus or conviction?

Despite all her claims to the contrary, Mrs Thatcher was not always always a conviction politician; she made U-turns and she pursued alternatives, sometimes willingly, sometimes unwillingly. Some of her ideas were borrowed; some were adapted; some were her own; and others were simply responses to changed circumstances.

In regard to environmental policy, there is little question that she responded to outside stimuli rather than taking a pioneering stance. Throughout the apparent metamorphosis that took her from describing the environment as a "humdrum" issue (1982) to referring to protecting the balance of nature as "one of the great challenges of the late twentieth century" (1988), she proposed no original approaches to environmental policy. She apparently did little more than simply tolerate the environmental lobby, acknowledging its existence, but neither proving particularly hostile to it, nor seeking to hear its views, nor offering to incorporate its ideas into the policy process. There was little to suggest that she really understood the environment as a policy issue. She revealed no particular convictions on the environment (beyond the simplistic argument that environmental regulation is an unwelcome handicap to economic development), and appears to have "discovered" the environment rather late in her political career.

Throughout the 1980s, the environmental lobby remained the active opposition on environmental issues, and was critical as much of the values of British society as it was of the specific priorities of the Thatcher government. The lobby was not extensively consulted by the Thatcher administration, and yet it brought about often significant policy changes, through either parliamentary activity, activity at the European Community level or the promotion of continuing changes in public attitudes. What the relationship between the environmental lobby and Thatcherism showed most clearly was that consensus and consultation did not end in British politics in 1979, and that Mrs Thatcher, for all her convictions, was often compelled to compromise.

(5) Is the environment a major policy issue in Britain?

Here the answer is uncertain. In 1980, neither the government nor the main opposition parties took the issue seriously, and none had an environmental policy, nor a coherent set of positions on particular issues. Environmental law was patchy, and the methods used to protect and manage the environment were largely held hostage to the wishes of vested economic interests, particularly the business, transport and agricultural lobbies. The network of government environmental agencies was incoherent, confused and largely ineffective. The environmental lobby was big and active, but it was politically marginalized. For many people, "the environment" meant simply protection of the countryside. Among political scientists, almost no attention was paid to the environment as a political or a policy issue.

By 1990, few in either government or the civil service showed much understanding of the importance of environmental management. Despite Thatcherite rhetoric, Thatcherite action was hesitant and conditional, and the much-heralded white paper proved hugely disappointing to the environmental lobby. The major opposition parties were beginning to claim improved green credentials, but none could claim a coherent environmental policy. The loss by the German Greens of all their seats in the December 1990 Bundestag elections was interpreted by some as a sign that the major German parties had stolen the environmental credentials of the Greens, and that green parties elsewhere in Europe should take heed. But it is still too early to be sure, least of all in Britain, where neither of the major parties can really claim to be green.

As this book goes to press, John Major has succeeded Margaret Thatcher, and shows signs (in some areas) of being more moderate than his predecessor. Michael Heseltine immediately returned to the cabinet with the environment portfolio, but local government was again his priority. There is still little sign that Britain – under the Conservatives or Labour – will move into the first rank of environmental achievers, alongside Germany, the Netherlands and the Scandinavians. Political scientists still pay almost no attention to the environment, nor to studying possible improvements in designing and implementing environmental policy.

The legacy of Thatcherism – at least in the short term – has been to create a new enterprise culture which has made explicit the underlying tensions between economic development and environmental management. Margaret Thatcher's policies made more clear the weaknesses of the institutional and legal structure of environmental policy in Britain. Finally, by showing up these weaknesses, they also emphasized the strength and importance of the British environmental lobby. In the absence of a coherent response by the British government to the environment, the lobby will continue to be the only effective force for positive and rational environmental protection.

Notes

1. Environmental policy in Britain

1. Kavanagh, Dennis and Anthony Seldon (eds), *The Thatcher Effect* (Oxford: Clarendon Press, 1989).
2. Blowers, Andrew, "Transition or transformation? Environmental policy under Thatcher", *Public Administration* 65 (autumn 1987), pp. 277–94.
3. Smith, Robert Angus, *Air and Rain: The Beginnings of a Chemical Climatology* (London: Longmans, Green, 1872).
4. McCormick, John, *Acid Earth: The Global Threat of Acid Pollution* (London: Earthscan, 1989).
5. Braybrooke, David and Charles E Lindblom, *A Strategy of Decision* (New York: Free Press, 1963), p. 71.
6. Lowe, Philip and Andrew Flynn, "Environmental politics and policy in the 1980s", in J. Mohan (ed.), *The Political Geography of Contemporary Britain* (London: Macmillan, 1989), p. 254.
7. Jordan, A. G. and J. J. Richardson, *British Politics and the Policy Process* (London: Allen & Unwin, 1987), p. ix.
8. O'Riordan, Timothy, "The politics of environmental regulation in Great Britain", *Environment*, 30, 8 (October 1988), pp. 5–9, 39–44.
9. Tinker, Jon, "Britain's environment: Nanny knows best", *New Scientist*, 53, 786 (9 March 1972), p. 530.
10. Royal Commission on Environmental Pollution, *Second Annual Report* (London: HMSO, 1972).
11. Friends of the Earth, *The Environment: The Government's Record* (London: FoE, 1989).
12. See e.g. Pye-Smith, Charlie and Chris Rose, *Crisis and Conserva-*

tion (Harmondsworth: Penguin, 1984); and MacEwen, Ann and Malcolm MacEwen, *National Parks: Conservation or Cosmetics?* (London: Allen & Unwin, 1982).
13. Council for the Protection of Rural England, *Annual Report 1989* (London: CPRE, 1989), p. 5
14. Pye-Smith and Rose, op. cit. (note 12), pp. 45, 83.
15. Kavanagh, Dennis, *British Politics: Continuities and Change* (Oxford: Oxford University Press, 1985), p. 152.
16. Jordan, A. G. and J. J. Richardson, *Government and Pressure Groups in Britain* (Oxford: Clarendon Press, 1987), pp. 3–4.
17. Ibid., p. 277.
18. Beer, Samuel, *Modern British Politics* (London: Faber, 1969), p. 71.
19. Ibid., p. 74.
20. Jordan and Richardson, op. cit. (note 16).
21. Marsh, David (ed.), *Pressure Politics: Interest Groups in Britain* (London: Junction Books, 1983), p. 15.
22. Grant, Wynn, "Insider groups, outsider groups and interest group strategies in Britain", Working Paper No. 19, May 1978, University of Warwick.
23. Jordan and Richardson, op. cit. (note 16), p. 187.
24. Hood, C., "Government bodies and government growth", in A. Barker (ed.), *Quangos in Britain* (Basingstoke: Macmillan, 1982).
25. Wilson, Andy (assistant secretary [policy], CPRE), personal communication, 1989.
26. Lowe, Philip and Jane Goyder, *Environmental Groups in Politics* (London: Allen & Unwin, 1983), p. 58.
27. O'Riordan, op. cit. (note 8).
28. Lowe and Flynn, op. cit. (note 6).
29. Lowe and Goyder, op. cit. (note 26), p. 62.
30. Ibid., pp. 64–5.
31. Ibid., p. 68.

2. The environmental lobby

1. Berry, Jeffrey M., *The Interest Group Society* (Boston: Little, Brown, 1984), p. 6.
2. Madgwick, P. J., *Introduction to British Politics* (London: Hutchinson, 1984), p. 308.
3. Finer, S. E., *Anonymous Empire* (London: Pall Mall, 1966), p. 3.

4. Thomas, Keith, *Man and the Natural World: Changing Attitudes in England 1500–1800* (Harmondsworth: Penguin, 1983).
5. Lowe, Philip, "Values and institutions in the history of British nature conservation", in Andrew Warren and Frank Goldsmith (eds.), *Conservation in Perspective* (Chichester: Wiley, 1983).
6. Sheail, John, *Nature in Trust* (London: Blackie, 1976), p. 4.
7. Ibid., p. 9.
8. Allen, David Elliston, *The Naturalist in Britain* (Harmondsworth: Penguin, 1978), pp. 197–8.
9. Lowe, op. cit. (note 5).
10. Sheail, op. cit. (note 6), p. 60.
11. McCormick, John, *The Global Environmental Movement* (London: Belhaven Press, 1989).
12. Lowe, Philip and Jane Goyder, *Environmental Groups in Politics* (London: Allen & Unwin, 1983), p. 1.
13. Frisch, Monica, *Directory for the Environment* (London: Green Print, 1990).
14. Stewart, J. D., *British Pressure Groups* (Oxford: Clarendon Press, 1958).
15. Marsh, David (ed.), *Pressure Politics: Interest Groups in Britain* (London: Junction Books, 1983).
16. Moran, M., *Politics and Society in Britain* (London: Macmillan, 1985).
17. Lowe and Goyder, op. cit. (note 12), p. 35.
18. Porritt, Jonathon (former Director, Friends of the Earth), personal communication, 1989.
19. McDonald, Peter (secretary, Wildlife Link), personal communication, 1990.
20. Burke, Tom (director, Green Alliance, and co-founder, Sustain-Ability), personal communication, 1989.
21. Jordan, A. G., and J. J. Richardson, *British Politics and the Policy Process* (London: Allen & Unwin, 1987), p. ix.
22. Crossman, Richard, *The Diaries of a Cabinet Minister*, Vol. 1 (London: Hamish Hamilton/Jonathan Cape, 1975).
23. Herman, Valentine and James Alt (eds), *Cabinet Studies* (London: Macmillan, 1975).
24. Mackintosh, J. P., *The British Cabinet* (London: Stevens & Sons, 1977).
25. Miller, Charles, *Lobbying Government* (Oxford: Blackwell, 1987), pp. 95–6.
26. Porritt, loc. cit. (note 18).

27. Frisch, op. cit. (note 13).
28. Ibid.
29. Moran, op. cit. (note 16), pp. 117–18.
30. Jordan, A. G. and J. J. Richardson, *Government and Pressure Groups in Britain* (Oxford: Clarendon Press, 1987), p. 235.
31. Lowe and Goyder, op.cit. (note 12).
32. Haigh, Nigel (director, IEEP London), personal communication, 1990.
33. Miller, op. cit. (note 25), p. 107.
34. Lowe and Goyder, op. cit. (note 12), pp. 68–9.
35. Porritt, loc. cit. (note 18).
36. Gammell, Alistair (director, international office, RSPB), personal communication, 1990.
37. Jordan and Richardson, op. cit. (note 30), pp. 251–2.
38. Jordan and Richardson, op. cit. (note 21), pp. 37–8.
39. Lowe and Goyder, op. cit. (note 12), pp. 74–6.

3. Thatcherism and the environment

1. Kavanagh, Dennis, *Thatcherism and British Politics: The End of Consensus?* (Oxford: Oxford University Press, 1987), pp. 2, 9.
2. Marquand, David, "The paradoxes of Thatcherism", in Robert Skidelsky (ed.), *Thatcherism* (London: Chatto & Windus, 1988), pp. 160–64.
3. Kavanagh, op. cit. (note 1), p. 13.
4. Holmes, Martin, *Thatcherism: Scope and Limits, 1983–87* (New York: St Martin's Press, 1989), p. 153.
5. Jenkins, Peter, *Mrs Thatcher's Revolution* (London: Pan, 1987), p. 81.
6. Lowe, Philip (lecturer in countryside planning, University College, London), personal communications, 1989–90.
7. Riddell, Peter, *The Thatcher Decade* (Oxford: Blackwell, 1989), p. 91.
8. Lowe, loc. cit. (note 6).
9. King, Anthony, "Margaret Thatcher: the style of a Prime Minister", in Anthony King (ed.), *The British Prime Minister* (Durham: Duke University Press, 1985), pp. 97–8.
10. Ibid., p. 115.
11. Ibid., p. 116.
12. Young, Hugo, *One of Us* (London: Macmillan, 1989), p. 430.

13. Simon Jenkins, *The Times*, 31 March 1983.
14. King, op. cit. (note 9), p. 118.
15. Young, op. cit. (note 12), p. 430.
16. King, op. cit. (note 9), p. 122.
17. Ibid., p. 122.
18. Holmes, op. cit. (note 4), pp. 152–3.
19. King, op. cit. (note 9), p. 124.
20. Ibid., p. 126.
21. Ibid., p. 137.
22. Edward Heath quoted in Sampson, Anthony, *The Changing Anatomy of Britain* (London: Hodder, 1982), p. 37.
23. Jenkins, op. cit. (note 5), p. 3.
24. Holmes, op. cit. (note 4), pp. 14, 18.
25. Jordan, A. G., and J. J. Richardson, *British Politics and the Policy Process* (London: Allen & Unwin 1987), p. ix.
26. Ibid., pp. 80–81.
27. Rose, Richard, *Do Parties Make a Difference?* (London: Macmillan, 1984).
28. Butler, David and Dennis Kavanagh, *The British General Election of 1987* (New York: St Martin's Press, 1988), p. 5.
29. Kavanagh, op. cit. (note 1), p. vii.
30. Marquand, op. cit. (note 2), p. 160.
31. Robert Skidelsky, *Guardian*, 21 September 1987.
32. Finer, S. E., *Thatcherism: Personality and Politics* (London: Macmillan, 1987), pp. 128–9.
33. *Observer*, 25 February 1979.
34. Kavanagh, op. cit. (note 1), p. 7.
35. Jenkins, op. cit. (note 5), p. 50.
36. Young, op. cit. (note 12), p. 223.
37. King, op. cit. (note 9), pp. 99–100.
38. Jenkins, op. cit. (note 5), pp. 50–51.
39. Beer, Samuel, *Modern British Politics* (London: Faber, 1969), p. 8.
40. Beer, Samuel, *Britain Against Itself* (New York: Norton, 1982).
41. Young, op. cit. (note 12), p. 273.
42. Burke, Tom (director, Green Alliance, and co-founder, Sustain-Ability), personal communication, 1989.
43. Murie, Alan, "Housing and the environment", in Denis Kavanaugh and Anthony Seldon (eds.), *The Thatcher Effect* (Oxford: Clarendon Press, 1989), p. 224.
44. Geoffrey Lean, *Observer*, 24 December 1989.
45. Thatcher, Margaret, *The Revival of Britain* (London: Aurum Press,

1989), p. 274.
46. Pearce, David, Anil Markandya and Edward Barbier, *Blueprint for a Green Economy* (London: Earthscan, 1989; the Pearce Report).
47. Jacques, Martin, "Why Thatcher turned green", *Sunday Times*, 2 October 1988.
48. Burke, loc. cit. (note 42).
49. Ratcliffe, Derek, "NCC: a difficult year", in BANC/Media Natura, *Ground Truth: A Report on the Prime Minister's First Green Year* (London: Media Natura, 1989).
50. *Economist*, 19 May 1990.
51. Porritt, Jonathon (former director, Friends of the Earth), personal communication, 1989; Haigh, Nigel (director, IEEP London), personal communication, 1990.
52. Burke, loc. cit. (note 42).
53. Jacques, op. cit. (note 47).
54. Burke, loc. cit. (note 42).
55. Wilson, Andy (assistant secretary [policy], CPRE), personal communication, 1989.
56. Baldock, David (senior fellow, IEEP), personal communication, 1989.
57. Porritt, loc. cit. (note 51).
58. Young, op. cit. (note 12), pp. 224–5.
59. Murie, op. cit. (note 43), p. 222.
60. Baldock, loc. cit. (note 56).
61. Burke, op. cit. (note 42).
62. Ibid.; Baldock, loc. cit. (note 56); Corrie, Heather (policy unit, World Wide Fund for Nature), personal communication, 1989; Porritt, loc. cit. (note 51).
63. Porritt, loc. cit. (note 51).
64. Baldock, loc. cit. (note 56).
65. Haigh, loc. cit. (note 51).
66. Friends of the Earth, *The Environment: The Government's Record* (London: FoE, 1989).
67. BANC/Media Natura, op. cit. (note 49).
68. Wilson, loc. cit. (note 55).
69. Burke, loc. cit. (note 42).

4. Environmental groups and the countryside

1. Shoard, Marion, *This Land Is Our Land* (London: Paladin 1987),

p. 103.

2. Munton, Richard, "Agriculture and conservation: what room for compromise?", in Andrew Warren and Frank Goldsmith (eds), *Conservation in Perspective* (Chichester: Wiley, 1983).
3. Westmacott, Richard and Tom Worthington, *New Agricultural Landscapes* (Cheltenham: Countryside Commission, 1974).
4. Shoard, op. cit. (note 1), p. 99.
5. Body, Richard, *Agriculture: The Triumph and the Shame* (London: Temple Smith, 1982), p. 3.
6. Howarth, Richard, *Farming for Farmers?* (London: Institute of Economic Affairs, 1985).
7. Pye-Smith, Charlie and Chris Rose, *Crisis and Conservation* (Harmondsworth: Penguin, 1984), pp. 4–5.
8. Howarth, op. cit. (note 6).
9. Shoard, op. cit. (note 1), p. 101.
10. Ibid., pp. 101–2.
11. Lowe, Philip, Graham Cox, Malcolm MacEwen, Tim O'Riordan and Michael Winter, *Countryside Conflicts: The Politics of Farming, Forestry and Conservation* (Aldershot: Gower, 1986), p. 134.
12. Adams, W. M., (department of geography, Downing College, Cambridge), personal communication, 1990.
13. Lowe *et al.*, op. cit. (note 11), pp. 152–3.
14. Cox, Graham, Philip Lowe and Michael Winter, "Agriculture and conservation in Britain: a policy community under siege", in Cox, Lowe and Winter (eds), *Agriculture: People and Policies* (London: Allen & Unwin, 1986).
15. Philip Lowe, quoted in Davies, Malcolm, *Politics of Pressure* (London: BBC Books, 1985).
16. Cox *et al*, op. cit. (note 14).
17. Jordan, A. G. and J. J. Richardson, *Government and Pressure Groups in Britain* (Oxford: Clarendon Press, 1987), pp. 110–11.
18. Wilson, Graham, *Special Interests and Policymaking* (London: Wiley, 1977), p. 35.
19. Ibid., p. 40.
20. Des Wilson quoted in Davies, op. cit. (note 15).
21. Jordan and Richardson, op. cit. (note 17), p. 36.
22. Shoard, op. cit. (note 1), p. 104.
23. Ibid., p. 123.
24. Finer, S. E., *Anonymous Empire* (London: Pall Mall, 1966), p. 38.
25. Jordan and Richardson, op. cit. (note 17), p. 113.
26. Wilson, loc. cit. (note 20).

27. Cox *et al*, op. cit. (note 14).
28. Ibid.
29. Ibid.
30. Ibid.
31. House of Lords Select Committee on the European Communities, *Agriculture and the Environment*. House of Lords Session 1983–4, 20th report. HL 272.
32. House of Lords Select Committee on Science and Technology, *Agriculture and Environmental Research*. House of Lords Session 1983–4, 4th report. HL 272.
33. House of Commons Environment Committee, *Operation and Effectiveness of Part II of the Wildlife and Countryside Act*, House of Commons Session 1984–5, 1st report. HC 6-11.
34. *Economist*, 19 May 1990, p. 68.
35. Adams, loc. cit. (note 12).

5. Privatization and pollution

1. Evelyn, John, *Fumifugium: or the Inconvenience of the Aer and Smoake of London: Two Prophecies* (New York: Maxwell Reprint Co., 1969).
2. Russell, Rollo, *London Fogs* (London: E Stanford, 1880).
3. Brimblecombe, Peter, *The Big Smoke* (London: Routledge, 1987), p. 124.
4. Ashby, Eric and Mary Anderson, *The Politics of Clean Air* (Oxford: Clarendon Press, 1981).
5. Enloe, Cynthia, *The Politics of Pollution in a Comparative Perspective* (New York: David Mackay, 1975), p. 25.
6. Elsom, Derek, *Atmospheric Pollution* (Oxford: Blackwell, 1987), p. 197.
7. Enloe, op. cit. (note 5), pp. 25–6.
8. DoE figures quoted in Elsom, op. cit. (note 6), p. 204.
9. Ashby and Anderson, op. cit. (note 4), p. 116.
10. Vogel, David, *National Styles of Regulation* (Ithaca: Cornell University Press, 1986), p. 78.
11. O'Riordan, Tim, "The role of environmental quality objectives: The politics of pollution control", in Tim O'Riordan and Ralph D'Arge (eds), *Progress in Resource Management and Environmental Planning* (New York: Wiley, 1979).
12. Ashby and Anderson, op. cit. (note 4), p. 34.

13. Scarrow, Howard, "The impact of British domestic air pollution legislation", *British Journal of Political Science*, 2, 3 (July 1972), p. 282.
14. Vogel, op. cit. (note 10), p. 79.
15. Elsom, op. cit. (note 6), p. 195.
16. Vogel, op. cit. (note 10), p. 101.
17. Lowe, Philip and Andrew Flynn, "Environmental politics and policy in the 1980s", in J. Mohan (ed.), *The Political Geography of Contemporary Britain* (London: Macmillan, 1989).
18. Jenkins, Simon, "Struggling in a nice stretch of water", *Sunday Times*, 12 March 1989.
19. Jenkins, Peter, *Mrs Thatcher's Revolution* (London: Pan, 1987), p. 370.
20. Kavanagh, Dennis, *Thatcherism and British Politics: The End of Consensus?* (Oxford: Oxford University Press, 1987), p. 223.
21. Wilson, Andy (assistant secretary [policy], CPRE), personal communication, 1989.
22. Friends of the Earth, *The Environment: The Government's Record* (London: FoE, 1989), pp. 68–9.
23. Wilson, loc. cit. (note 21).
24. *Economist*, 1 October 1988.
25. Skea, James, *Electricity for Life? Choices for the Environment* (London: CPRE/FoE, 1988).
26. Council for the Protection of Rural England, Friends of the Earth, World Wide Fund for Nature and Association for the Conservation of Energy, *Greening the Bill* (London: CPRE/FoE/WWF/ACE, 1989).
27. National Society for Clean Air, *1988–89 Annual Report* (Brighton: NSCA, 1989), p. 8.
28. Gribben, John, *The Hole in the Sky* (New York: Bantam, 1988).
29. Friends of the Earth, op. cit. (note 22), p. 56.

6. The new green society

1. Market and Opinion Research International, *The Greening Consumer* (London: MORI, 1989).
2. Parkin, Sara, *Green Parties: An International Guide* (London: Heretic Books, 1989).
3. Galbraith, John Kenneth, *The Affluent Society* (London: Hamish Hamilton, 1958).

4. See e.g. Swatek, Paul, *The User's Guide to the Protection of the Environment* (San Francisco: FoE, 1970); and Holliman, Jonathan, *Consumer's Guide to the Protection of the Environment* (London: Pan/Ballantine, 1971).
5. McCormick, John, *The User's Guide to the Environment* (London: Kogan Page, 1985).
6. *Economist*, 21 July 1990.
7. Elkington, John (executive director, SustainAbility), personal communication, 1989.
8. Nicholson, Max (founder, ENDS), personal communication, 1982.
9. Elkington, John, Tom Burke and Julia Hailes, *Green Pages: The Business of Saving the World* (London: Routledge, 1988).
10. Elkington, loc. cit. (note 7).
11. Anita Roddick quoted in Elkington, John and Julia Hailes, *The Green Consumer Guide* (London: Gollancz, 1988).
12. Crewe, Ivor, "Values: the crusade that failed", in Denis Kavanagh and Anthony Seldon (eds), *The Thatcher Effect* (Oxford: Clarendon Press, 1989), p. 241.
13. MORI, in *British Public Opinion*, 10, 6 (July–August 1988).
14. *Economist*, 10 March 1990.
15. Friends of the Earth, *The Aerosol Connection* (London: FoE, 1988).
16. Elkington, op. cit. (note 7).
17. Burke, Tom (director, Green Alliance, and co-founder, Sustain-Ability), personal communication, 1989.
18. Elkington, op. cit. (note 7).
19. Burke, loc. cit. (note 17).
20. Tydeman, Chris (World Wide Fund for Nature), personal communication, 1989.
21. Porritt, Jonathon (former director, Friends of the Earth), personal communication, 1989.
22. Ibid.
23. Ibid.
24. Lowe, Philip and Jane Goyder, *Environmental Groups in Politics* (London: Allen & Unwin, 1983).
25. Lowe, Philip (lecturer in countryside planning, University College, London), personal communications, 1989–90.
26. World Wide Fund for Nature, *WWF Review 1989* (Godalming: WWF, 1989), p. 20.
27. Lowe, loc. cit. (note 25).
28. Elkington, loc. cit. (note 7).

29. Parkin, op. cit. (note 2).
30. Lowe, loc. cit. (note 25).
31. Parkin, op. cit. (note 2).
32. Lowe, loc. cit. (note 25).
33. Chittenden, Maurice and Andrew Grice, "The pub party blossoms forth", *Sunday Times*, 25 June 1990.
34. Lowe, loc. cit. (note 25).
35. Jacques, Martin, "Change of pace puts the Tories out of step", *Sunday Times*, 2 July 1989.
36. Chittenden and Grice, op. cit. (note 33).
37. Kilroy-Silk, Robert, "Brief summer of the Greens", *The Times*, 29 September 1989.
38. Chittenden and Grice, op. cit. (note 33).
39. Ibid.

7. The environment and the European Community

1. Farquhar, J. T., "The policies of the European Community towards the environment – the "dangerous substances" directive", *Journal of Planning and Environmental Law*, March 1983, pp. 145–55.
2. Haigh, Nigel, *EEC Environmental Policy and Britain* (London: ENDS, 1984).
3. Ibid.
4. Haigh, Nigel, "Devolved responsibility and centralization: effects of EEC environmental policy", *Public Administration*, 64, 2 (summer 1986), pp. 197–207.
5. Haigh, Nigel (director, IEEP London), personal communication, 1990.
6. Ibid.
7. Lowe, Philip and Andrew Flynn, "Environmental politics and policy in the 1980s", in J. Mohan (ed.), *The Political Geography of Contemporary Britain* (London: Macmillan, 1989).
8. Daltrop, Anne, *Politics and the European Community* (Harlow: Longman, 1986), p. 185.
9. Lowe, Philip (lecturer in countryside planning, University College, London), personal communications, 1989–90.
10. Daltrop, op. cit. (note 8).
11. Baldock, David (senior fellow, IEEP), personal communication, 1989; Lowe, loc. cit. (note 9).
12. Lowe, loc. cit. (note 9).

13. Baldock, loc. cit. (note 11).
14. Lowe, loc. cit. (note 9).
15. Baldock, loc. cit. (note 11).
16. Gammell, Alistair (director, international office, RSPB), personal communication, 1990.
17. Haigh, loc. cit. (note 5).
18. Daltrop, op. cit. (note 8).
19. Lowe, Philip and Jane Goyder, *Environmental Groups in Politics* (London: Allen & Unwin, 1983), pp. 175–6.
20. Haigh, loc. cit. (note 5).
21. Ibid.
22. Baldock, loc. cit. (note 11).
23. Wilson, Des, *Pressure: The A to Z of Campaigning in Britain* (London: Heinemann, 1984).
24. Haigh, loc. cit. (note 5).
25. Wilson, op. cit. (note 23), p. 156.
26. Ibid., p. 179.
27. Elsom, Derek, *Atmospheric Pollution* (Oxford: Blackwell, 1987), p. 216.
28. Haigh, op. cit. (note 2), p. 186.
29. Haigh, Nigel, "Public perceptions and international influences", in Gordon Conway (ed.), *The Assessment of Environmental Problems* (London: Imperial College, Centre for Environmental Technology, 1986), p. 81.
30. Haigh, loc. cit. (note 5).
31. Haigh, op. cit. (note 29), p. 82.
32. Haigh, loc. cit. (note 5).
33. Royal Commission on Environmental Pollution, *Annual Report* (London: HMSO, 1984).
34. House of Commons Environment Committee, *Fourth Report: Acid Rain* (London: HMSO, 1984); House of Lords Select Committee on the European Communities, *22nd Report: Air Pollution* (London: HMSO, 1984).
35. Bow Publications, *A Role for Britain in the Acid Rainstorm* (London: Bow Publications, 1984).
36. Fry, Garry, Ivar Muniz and Arnie Semb, "Nice video, shame about the fish", *New Scientist*, 27 March 1986, pp. 46–7.
37. Committee on Air Pollution (Beaver Committee), *Report*, Cmnd 9322 (London: HMSO, November 1954).
38. UK Review Group on Acid Rain, *Acid Deposition in the United Kingdom* (Stevenage: Warren Spring Laboratory, 1984).

39. UN Economic Commission for Europe, *National Strategies and Policies for Air Pollution Abatement* (New York: United Nations, 1987).
40. Wetstone, Gregory S. and Armin Rosencranz, *Acid Rain in Europe and North America: National Responses to an International Problem* (Washington: Environmental Law Institute, 1983).

8. The changing environmental lobby

1. O'Riordan, Timothy, "The politics of environmental regulation in Great Britain", *Environment*, 30, 8 (October 1988), pp. 5–9, 39–44.
2. *Sunday Times*, 30 June 1989.
3. *Economist*, 3 March 1990.
4. Wilson, Andy (assistant secretary [policy], CPRE), personal communication, 1989.
5. Council for the Protection of Rural England, *Annual Report 1988* (London: CPRE, 1988), p. 18.
6. O'Reilly, Emma Louise (National Trust), personal communication, 1989.
7. Mattingly, Alan (director, Ramblers' Association), personal communication, 1990.
8. Haigh, Nigel (director, IEEP London), personal communication, 1990.
9. Skea, James, *Electricity for Life? Choices for the Environment* (London: CPRE/FoE, 1988).
10. Porritt, Jonathon (former director, Friends of the Earth), personal communication, 1989.
11. Ibid.
12. Ibid.
13. CPRE, op. cit. (note 5), p. 24.
14. Porritt, loc. cit. (note 10).
15. National Society for Clean Air, *1988–89 Annual Report* (Brighton: NSCA, 1989).
16. Melchett, Peter (executive director, Greenpeace), personal communication, 1990.
17. Rose, Chris (director, Media Natura), personal communication, 1990.
18. Pye-Smith, Charlie and Chris Rose, *Crisis and Conservation* (Harmondsworth: Penguin, 1984), pp. 183–4.

19. *The Times*, 13 July 1989.
20. World Wildlife Fund, *Annual Report 1986* (Godalming: WWF, 1986).
21. Medley, George (director, World Wide Fund for Nature), personal communication, 1989.
22. Mattingly, loc. cit. (note 7).
23. Porritt, loc. cit. (note 10).
24. Adams, W. M. (department of geography, Downing College, Cambridge), personal communication, 1990.

9. Environmental politics in Britain

1. *The Times*, 26 September 1990.
2. *The Times*, 24 September 1990.
3. *The Times*, 26 September 1990.
4. Ibid.
5. Hirst, Paul, *After Thatcher* (London: Collins, 1989), p. 11.
6. Riddell, Peter, *The Thatcher Decade* (Oxford: Blackwell, 1989), p. 2.
7. Riddell, Peter, *The Thatcher Government* (Oxford: Blackwell, 1985).
8. Riddell, op. cit. (note 6), p. 75.
9. Ibid., p. 118.
10. Ibid., p. 115.

Index